HEINEMANN MATHEMATICS P7

Textbook

These are the different types of pages and symbols used in this book and associated workbooks.

1
Mental addition and subtraction

Most textbook and workbook pages are of this type. They deal with mathematical concepts, skills and applications in number, measure, shape and handling data.

59
Other activity: mental calculation, money

These pages provide self-contained activities which need not necessarily be tackled in the order in which they are presented. They are intended to give further opportunities for children to apply the mathematics they have learned or to extend their experience.

Problem solving

Some pages, or parts of a page, provide an opportunity for problem solving or investigative work.

Where a calculator would be useful this is indicated by a calculator symbol.

This symbol indicates that more work of this kind can be found on the numbered Reinforcement Sheet.

The numbered Home Link-up activity gives further practice in this work.

Heinemann Educational, Halley Court,
Jordan Hill, Oxford OX2 8EJ
a division of Reed Educational and Professional Publishing Ltd

Designed by Miller, Craig and Cocking
Produced by Oxprint
Printed in the UK by Bath Colour Books, Glasgow

First Published 1996   ISBN 0 435 02248 2

99 98 97 96

10 9 8 7 6 5 4 3 2

Contents

Homework activities for these pages are provided in Home Link-up.

Measure

		Textbook	Workbook	Reinf't Sheets	Extension Textbook
Length	Millimetres, scale	68–70*	15	22, 23	
	Perimeter, formulae	71*			
Weight	Kilograms and grams, kilograms and tonnes	72–74*			
Area	Rectangles, A = l × b, composite shapes	75, 76*		24	E16, E17
	Irregular shapes		24		
	Right-angled triangles, composite shapes	77*	25*, 26*	25, 26	
	Square metre, square kilometre	78	27		
Volume	Cuboids, V = l × b × h	79, 80*			
	Millilitres		28*		E19
Imperial units	Inches, feet, pounds, pints, gallons	81, 82			
Rate and Speed	Rate: per minute, per second	83, 84*			
	Speed: metres per second, kilometres per hour	85, 86*		27	E20
Time	12-hour clock, durations	87*			
	24-hour clock, durations	88*, 89*		28	E21
	24-hour clock, counting on, counting back	90*, 91*	16	29	
Other activity					E4

Shape

		Textbook	Workbook	Reinf't Sheets	Extension Textbook
Angles	Measuring, drawing, calculations	92*, 93*	29, 30	30	
	Bearings	94–6*			E22, E23
Symmetry and Tiling	Rotational symmetry	97	17		
	Tiling, translation	98	18, 20		E24
3D shape	Nets, faces, vertices, edges	99, 100			
2D shape	Sides and angles, diagonals, rigidity	101–104*		31	E25, E26
	Parallel lines	105*			
Other activities		106, 107, 117			E30

Handling data

		Textbook	Workbook	Reinf't Sheets	Extension Textbook
Handling data	Questionnaires	108			
	Bar graphs, combined bar graphs	109, 110*	31		
	Pie charts, trend graphs	111*, 112	32*		
	Range, median, mode, mean	113*			
	Frequency tables, class intervals	114*	33, 34*	32	
	Surveys	115, 116			E28, E29
Probability	Likelihood, probability scale	118–20*			
Context	Mixed mathematics	121–25	35, 36		

Record of Work grids

37–9

* *Homework activities for these pages are provided in Home Link-up.*

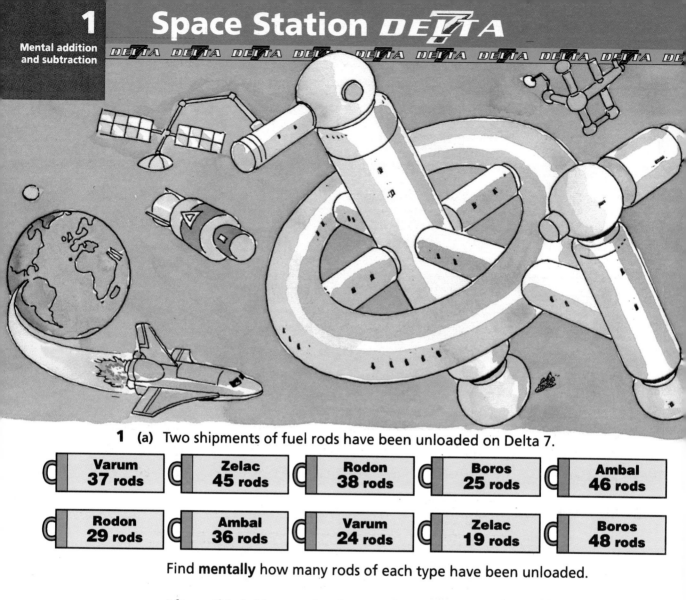

1 (a) Two shipments of fuel rods have been unloaded on Delta 7.

Varum 37 rods	Zelac 45 rods	Rodon 38 rods	Boros 25 rods	Ambal 46 rods

Rodon 29 rods	Ambal 36 rods	Varum 24 rods	Zelac 19 rods	Boros 48 rods

Find **mentally** how many rods of each type have been unloaded.

(b) After a third shipment has been unloaded there are 90 rods of each type. What type of fuel is in each of these containers?

17 rods	26 rods	29 rods

2 Subtract **mentally**.

(a) 68 – 35   (b) 87 – 32   (c) 98 – 23   (d) 72 – 61   (e) 89 – 33

(f) 74 – 25   (g) 68 – 39   (h) 80 – 27   (i) 55 – 16   (j) 70 – 26

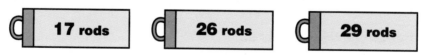

Ten of these calculations have answers greater than 60.

3 Is the droid telling the truth? Calculate mentally to find out.

(a) 19 + 23   (b) 26 + 27   (c) 28 + 36   (d) 47 + 17   (e) 26 + 26

(f) 53 – 17   (g) 80 – 19   (h) 93 – 24   (i) 84 – 47   (j) 81 – 33

(k) 44 + 23   (l) 84 – 51   (m) 41 + 29   (n) 58 + 13   (o) 60 – 22

(p) 67 – 48   (q) 16 + 49   (r) 85 – 46   (s) 34 + 39   (t) 96 – 27

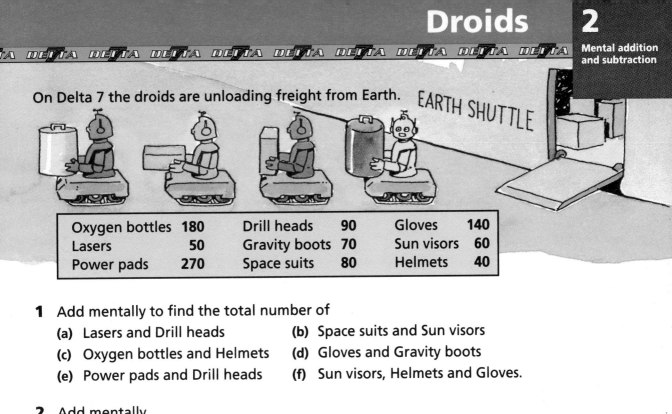

On Delta 7 the droids are unloading freight from Earth.

Oxygen bottles	180	Drill heads	90	Gloves	140
Lasers	50	Gravity boots	70	Sun visors	60
Power pads	270	Space suits	80	Helmets	40

1 Add mentally to find the total number of
- **(a)** Lasers and Drill heads
- **(b)** Space suits and Sun visors
- **(c)** Oxygen bottles and Helmets
- **(d)** Gloves and Gravity boots
- **(e)** Power pads and Drill heads
- **(f)** Sun visors, Helmets and Gloves.

2 Add mentally.
- **(a)** 76 + 50
- **(b)** 82 + 40
- **(c)** 90 + 55
- **(d)** 80 + 26
- **(e)** 30 + 99
- **(f)** 160 + 35
- **(g)** 120 + 39
- **(h)** 48 + 130
- **(i)** 72 + 120
- **(j)** 160 + 27
- **(k)** 180 + 54
- **(l)** 132 + 90
- **(m)** 80 + 145
- **(n)** 76 + 160
- **(o)** 180 + 99

3 The hatch to the [LOADING] bay is coded.

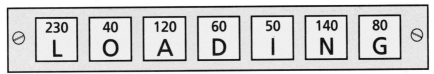

230	40	120	60	50	140	80
L	O	A	D	I	N	G

Find the difference between the numbers on buttons
- **(a)** A and D
- **(b)** L and G
- **(c)** N and I
- **(d)** A and O
- **(e)** L and A.

4 Which buttons did the droid press?
- **(a)** ☐ − ☐ = 100
- **(b)** ☐ − ☐ = 70
- **(c)** ☐ − ☐ = 170

5 Subtract mentally.
- **(a)** 150 − 44
- **(b)** 260 − 58
- **(c)** 280 − 72
- **(d)** 330 − 25
- **(e)** 470 − 61
- **(f)** 300 − 41
- **(g)** 290 − 49
- **(h)** 500 − 63
- **(i)** 160 − 19
- **(j)** 250 − 12
- **(k)** 140 − 23
- **(l)** 350 − 16
- **(m)** 250 − 29
- **(n)** 480 − 37
- **(o)** 370 − 42

6 Add mentally in the **easiest order** to find each droid's number. Write your order.
- **(a)** 8 35 2
- **(b)** 7 18 3
- **(c)** 25 20 5
- **(d)** 31 31 9
- **(e)** 16 14 26
- **(f)** 20 18 12
- **(g)** 19 21 30
- **(h)** 12 10 38

Go to Workbook page 1.

R1 H1

DELTA Ecolabs

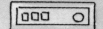

Dr Martha Thomas runs the food research laboratories.

Ecolab 1

Ecolab 2

This table shows the numbers of fruit in two of the Ecolabs.

	banapples	peacherries	lemoranges	plumpears	kiwiberries
Ecolab 1	2187	3081	1102	8230	9416
Ecolab 2	1343	793	657	3578	7807

1 Find the total number of each type of fruit in Ecolabs 1 and 2.

2 How many more of each type of fruit are there in Ecolab 1 than in Ecolab 2?

Ecolab 3 has twice as many banapples as Ecolab 1, 350 more lemoranges than Ecolab 2 and 945 fewer peacherries than Ecolab 1.
It has the same number of kiwiberries as plumpears.
There are 7997 fruits altogether.

Problem solving

3 How many of each type of fruit are there in Ecolab 3?

4 There are four Ecolabs. Find the number of each of these types of fruit in Ecolab 4.

	banapples	peacherries	lemoranges
Total number in all four Ecolabs	8793	7000	3060

Multi-grow TEST SAMPLE

Ingredients
minerals 4146 gg
.vitamins 325 gg
Nutross 6830 gg
Provak 72 gg

Dr Thomas has been experimenting with new plant foods.

1 Find the total weight, in galactograms (gg), of the ingredients in the Multi-grow test sample.

2 The weight of a caulipea fed with Multi-grow was recorded.

	Mon	Tue	Wed	Thu	Fri	Sat	Sun
Weight in galactograms	43	219	1422	2081	3185	4602	7158

Find the change in the caulipea's weight from
(a) Monday to Wednesday   (b) Tuesday to Thursday
(c) Wednesday to Friday   (d) Monday to Saturday
(e) Saturday to Sunday   (f) Tuesday to Sunday.

3 Dr Thomas sends samples of her experimental foods to Earth.

Batch 1	potatoflowers	3248	parsnibeans	1075
	carronips	643	turnipeas	30

Batch 2	carronips	615	radisprouts	72
	turnipeas	3924	caulipeas	136

Batch 3	radisprouts	95	parsnibeans	204
	potatoflowers	173	carronips	3827

(a) Find the total number of samples in each batch.

(b) How many more samples were sent in
   • batch 1 than in batch 2
   • batch 2 than in batch 3
   • batch 1 than in batch 3?

4 Three of Dr Thomas's oniotts weigh 9600 gg altogether. One oniott weighs 425 gg less than the heaviest and 425 gg more than the lightest. Find the weight of each oniott.

Problem solving

H2

Transporter *Zarco*

DELTA DELTA DELTA DELTA DELTA DELTA DELTA DELTA DELTA DE

Delta 7 sends supplies to the miners on Planet Stobal.

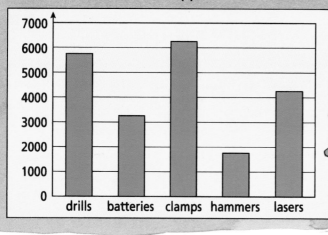

1 **To the nearest thousand**, write the number of

(a) drills   (b) batteries   (c) clamps   (d) hammers   (e) lasers.

2 Round **to the nearest thousand**.

(a) 3800   (b) 8240   (c) 7775   (d) 1909   (e) 5055   (f) 6995

(g) 14 205   (h) 18 628   (i) 11 991   (j) 28 505   (k) 39 099   (l) 41 099

(m) 15 515   (n) 46 600   (o) 22 499   (p) 73 775   (q) 33 500   (r) 59 955

3 These are the fuel tank readings from transporter *Zarco*.

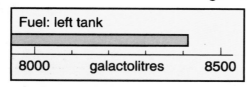

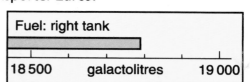

To the nearest hundred galactolitres, write the volume of fuel in each tank.

4 Round **to the nearest hundred**.

(a) 3608   (b) 9277   (c) 4099   (d) 13 299   (e) 47 607   (f) 21 341

(g) 22 155   (h) 35 055   (i) 15 555   (j) 40 040   (k) 18 848   (l) 58 550

Cargo weights in galactograms

Transporter *Zarco*: 5762

Transporter *Nina*: 2180

5762 is about 6000.
2180 is about 2000.

6000 + 2000 = 8000
The total weight is
about **8000 gg**.

5 Estimate.

(a) 3239 + 4943   (b) 1860 + 2107   (c) 8311 − 3984

(d) 14 632 − 8753   (e) 9355 + 14 602   (f) 26 505 − 3678

R2 H3

Go to Workbook page 2.

1 Droids stack fuel rods like this:

  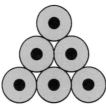 

Stack 1   Stack 2   Stack 3   Stack 4

(a) Draw the next two stacks.

(b) Copy and complete this table.

Stack	1	2	3	4	5	6	7	8
Number of rods	1	3						

(c) The number of rods in each stack is a **triangular number**.
Describe how to find the **ninth** triangular number.

2 Stacks of rods are slotted into square panels in the reactor.

  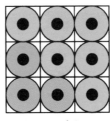 

panel 1   panel 2   panel 3

(a) Draw the next two panels.

(b) Copy and complete this table.

Panel	1	2	3	4	5	6	7	8
Number of rods	1	4						

(c) The number of rods in each panel is a **square number**.
Describe how to find the **ninth** square number.

1   3   6   10   15   21   28

3 (a) What do you notice about the sum of any two consecutive triangular numbers?

Problem solving

(b) Which two triangular numbers add to give the **tenth** square number?

4 91 and 105 are consecutive triangular numbers.
What is the next triangular number?

Problem solving

91   105   ?

Constructa and the Lineum Mine are work zones on Stobal.

1 Squad 1 follows the yellow route to Constructa.
- Multiply each number on the yellow route by 10.
- Write the rule you used for multiplying by 10.

2 Thermo-bricks are in stacks of ten. How many bricks are there in 1500 stacks?

3 Squad 2 follows the green route to the Lineum Mine.
- Multiply each number on the green route by 100.
- Write the rule you used for multiplying by 100.

4 A worker at Constructa earns 100 credits per day.
How many credits would she earn in 360 days?

5 Multiply each of these numbers by 1000.

(a) 75	(b) 83	(c) 90	(d) 105	(e) 186	(f) 213
(g) 250	(h) 272	(i) 390	(j) 584	(k) 1013	(l) 1230

6 Write a rule for multiplying by 1000.

7 Workers at Constructa loaded 1000 magno-pipes onto each truck. How many magno-pipes were loaded onto (a) 125 trucks (b) 200 trucks (c) 350 trucks?

BONUS
1000 credits for every 100 magno-pipes laid

8 Squad 1 laid 400 000 magno-pipes.
How many credits did they earn?

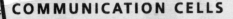
Squad 3 are preparing to explore an uncharted region.
They check that their equipment is complete.

COMMUNICATION CELLS

3 packs of 14 cells.

3 tens + 3 fours
= 30 + 12
= **42 cells**

1 Find mentally.

(a) 16 × 4 (b) 12 × 9
(c) 13 × 5 (d) 18 × 3
(e) 8 × 17 (f) 15 × 7
(g) 17 × 6 (h) 2 × 19
(i) 8 × 15 (j) 16 × 9
(k) 14 × 4 (l) 6 × 18

RATION PACKS

2 Find mentally.

(a) 7 × 20 (b) 8 × 90
(c) 6 × 60 (d) 40 × 5
(e) 60 × 9 (f) 7 × 70
(g) 4 × 80 (h) 50 × 3
(i) 30 × 6 (j) 9 × 70

8 boxes of 30 ration packs.

8 × 3 tens
= 24 tens
= **240 packs**

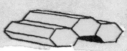

STERILISING TABLETS

5 bottles of 800 tablets.

5 × 8 hundreds
= 40 hundreds
= **4000 tablets**

3 Find mentally.

(a) 4 × 400   (b) 8 × 200
(c) 6 × 300   (d) 700 × 3
(e) 900 × 2   (f) 5 × 600
(g) 7 × 800   (h) 500 × 9
(i) 600 × 8   (j) 6 × 700
(k) 5 × 800   (l) 9 × 500

HEATING CUBES

4 Find mentally.

(a) 20 × 50 (b) 60 × 70
(c) 90 × 40 (d) 30 × 40
(e) 70 × 60 (f) 90 × 70
(g) 40 × 20 (h) 60 × 80
(i) 80 × 90 (j) 50 × 30

30 tubs of 40 cubes.

3 tens × 4 tens
= 12 hundreds
= **1200 cubes**

LIGHT CAPSULES

43 tins of 17 capsules.

43 is about 40.
17 is about 20.
40 × 20 = 800, so there
are **about 800 capsules.**

R3

H5

5 Estimate.

(a) 32 × 18 (b) 17 × 41 (c) 28 × 19 (d) 31 × 14 (e) 45 × 16 (f) 19 × 35

1 Workers at the lineum mine work in teams of 10.
How many teams of 10 can be made from

(a) 70 workers   (b) 90 workers   (c) 120 workers   (d) 2000 workers?

2 Write the rule you used for dividing by 10.

3 Find mentally, one tenth of

(a) 260   (b) 300   (c) 450   (d) 610   (e) 700
(f) 2050   (g) 4000   (h) 51 000   (i) 99 000   (j) 150 000

4 Each worker earns one credit for every 100 crystals mined.
How many credits does each of these workers earn?

	Crystals mined
Andy	9600
Karen	6500
Edwin	10 200
Sobia	13 800

	Crystals mined
Marina	5000
Paulo	12 000
Shamir	9900
Fians	10 000

5 Write the rule you used for dividing by 100.

6 Find mentally, one hundredth of

(a) 8200   (b) 3700   (c) 8000   (d) 33 300   (e) 720 000

7 How many super-credits will each of these miners earn?

BONUS PAYMENT
One super-credit for every 1000 crystals mined!

	Crystals mined
Helga	49 000
Ivan	583 000
Susan	60 000
Irena	480 000

	Crystals mined
Franco	601 000
Sonya	9000
Sven	90 000
Linton	900 000

8 Write a rule for dividing by 1000.

9 Find **mentally.**

(a) 2000 ÷ 1000   (b) 20 000 ÷ 1000   (c) 200 000 ÷ 1000
(d) 8000 ÷ 1000   (e) 80 000 ÷ 1000   (f) 808 000 ÷ 1000

10 Find **mentally.**

(a) 3500 ÷ 10   (b) 44 100 ÷ 100   (c) 31 000 ÷ 1000
(d) 29 000 ÷ 100   (e) 3000 ÷ 1000   (f) 9020 ÷ 10
(g) 700 000 ÷ 1000   (h) 400 000 ÷ 10   (i) 300 000 ÷ 100

The squads prepare to return to the space station.

240 ration packs are to be loaded into 8 containers.

240 divided by 8.
= 24 tens ÷ 8
=   3 tens
= 30 packs

1 **(a)** Find mentally, the number of packs in each container.

A 540 ÷ 6   **B** 200 ÷ 5   **C** 350 ÷ 7   **D** 360 ÷ 4

E 280 ÷ 4   **F** 180 ÷ 6   **G** 720 ÷ 8   **H** 600 ÷ 10

I 150 ÷ 3   **J** 100 ÷ 2   **K** 800 ÷ 10   **L** 560 ÷ 7

M 900 ÷ 10   **N** 630 ÷ 7   **O** 360 ÷ 9   **P** 700 ÷ 10

Q 360 ÷ 6   **R** 400 ÷ 5   **S** 490 ÷ 7   **T** 150 ÷ 5

(b) Which containers go in each buggy?
- answers which are multiples of 40 ⟶ red buggy
- answers which are multiples of 30 ⟶ yellow buggy
- other answers ⟶ blue buggy

2 **(a)** Copy this grid onto squared paper.
(b) Colour squares to show the positions of these space hazards.

400	140	180	640	450
150	420	560	900	810
210	880	630	800	160
490	110	700	250	540
270	320	480	430	300

 asteroids – numbers which have 8 as a factor

 meteors – numbers which have 9 as a factor

(c) List the numbers of the uncoloured squares to give the safe route home.

R4

H6

DELTA control . . .

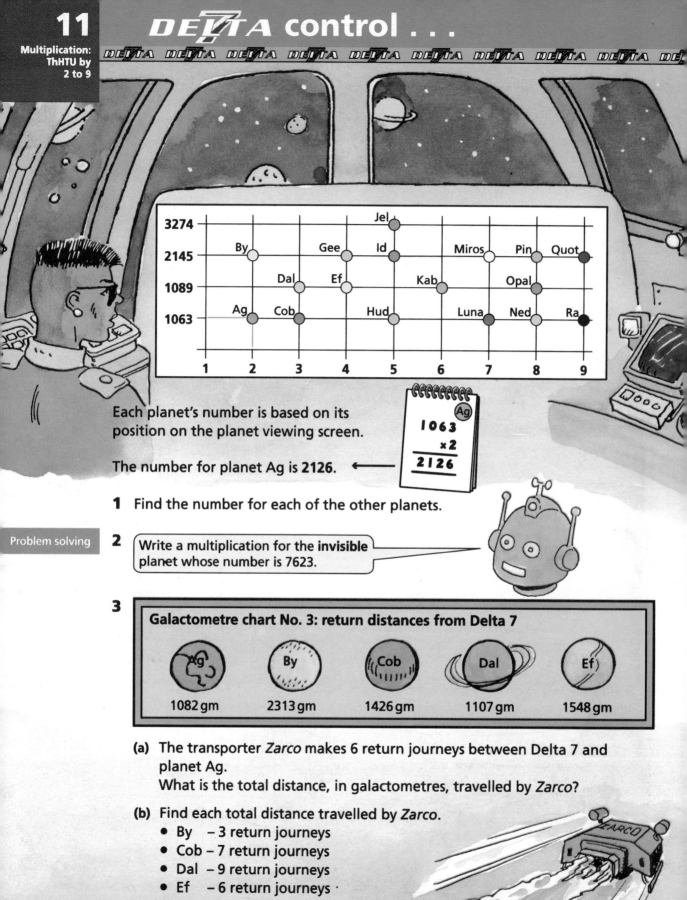

Each planet's number is based on its position on the planet viewing screen.

The number for planet Ag is **2126**.

$$\begin{array}{r} 1063 \\ \times 2 \\ \hline 2126 \end{array}$$

1 Find the number for each of the other planets.

2 Write a multiplication for the **invisible** planet whose number is 7623.

3

Galactometre chart No. 3: return distances from Delta 7

Ag	By	Cob	Dal	Ef
1082 gm	2313 gm	1426 gm	1107 gm	1548 gm

(a) The transporter *Zarco* makes 6 return journeys between Delta 7 and planet Ag.
What is the total distance, in galactometres, travelled by *Zarco*?

(b) Find each total distance travelled by *Zarco*.
- By – 3 return journeys
- Cob – 7 return journeys
- Dal – 9 return journeys
- Ef – 6 return journeys

(c) *Zarco* makes 1 return journey to one planet and 5 return journeys to another planet, travelling a total distance of 6961 galactometres.
Name the planets. Explain your answer.

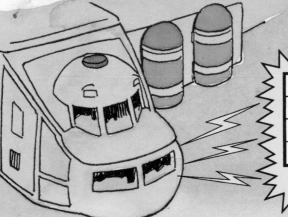

8771 ÷ 7	9684 ÷ 9	9380 ÷ 4	8832 ÷ 8
9915 ÷ 3	2142 ÷ 6	9535 ÷ 5	7842 ÷ 6
1428 ÷ 4	2092 ÷ 2		3213 ÷ 9
7911 ÷ 3	9783 ÷ 9	9149 ÷ 7	5230 ÷ 5
	6535 ÷ 5	9992 ÷ 8	9774 ÷ 6

1 Delta 7 transmits a message to the transporter *Zarco*.

(a) Find the answer to each calculation in the message.

(b) Use the **Galactic Code**. What is Delta 7's message?

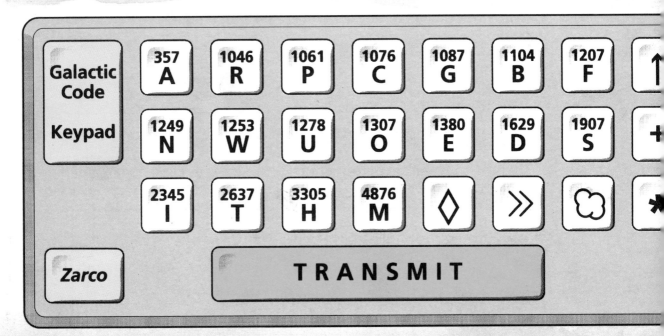

Galactic Code	**357** A	**1046** R	**1061** P	**1076** C	**1087** G	**1104** B	**1207** F ↑
Keypad	**1249** N	**1253** W	**1278** U	**1307** O	**1380** E	**1629** D	**1907** S +
	2345 I	**2637** T	**3305** H	**4876** M	◊	≫	✿ ✱

Zarco   **TRANSMIT**

2 What is *Zarco's* reply?

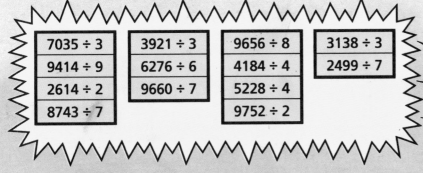

7035 ÷ 3	3921 ÷ 3	9656 ÷ 8	3138 ÷ 3
9414 ÷ 9	6276 ÷ 6	4184 ÷ 4	2499 ÷ 7
2614 ÷ 2	9660 ÷ 7	5228 ÷ 4	
8743 ÷ 7		9752 ÷ 2	

3 *Zarco's* captain made a mistake! The planet was Pu.
Make up divisions to give the Galactic Code for planet Pu.

Problem solving

H8

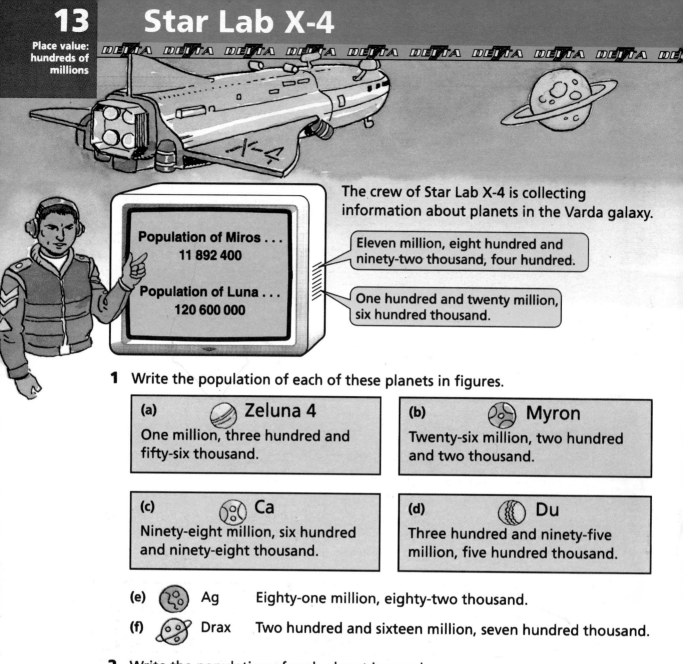

The crew of Star Lab X-4 is collecting information about planets in the Varda galaxy.

Population of Miros . . .
11 892 400

Eleven million, eight hundred and ninety-two thousand, four hundred.

Population of Luna . . .
120 600 000

One hundred and twenty million, six hundred thousand.

1 Write the population of each of these planets in figures.

(a) Zeluna 4
One million, three hundred and fifty-six thousand.

(b) Myron
Twenty-six million, two hundred and two thousand.

(c) Ca
Ninety-eight million, six hundred and ninety-eight thousand.

(d) Du
Three hundred and ninety-five million, five hundred thousand.

(e) Ag   Eighty-one million, eighty-two thousand.

(f) Drax   Two hundred and sixteen million, seven hundred thousand.

2 Write the population of each planet in words.

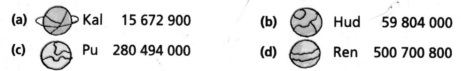

(a) Kal   15 672 900

(b) Hud   59 804 000

(c) Pu   280 494 000

(d) Ren   500 700 800

3 The displays show the number of Lineum crystals on each planet.
Write the value of each arrowed digit.

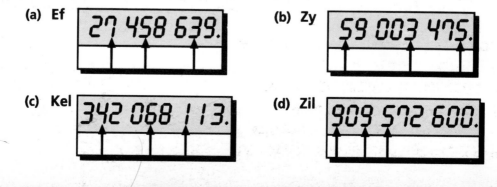

(a) Ef   27 458 639.

(b) Zy   59 003 475.

(c) Kel   342 068 113.

(d) Zil   909 572 600.

The monitors show the numbers of Rodon crystals on these planets.

Var	850 672.	Zol	3 117 290.	Hud	12 500 000.
Pu	20 200 200.	Ren	99 003 440.	Ra	756 305 070.
Ag	8 974 619.	Kal	118 803 652.	Va	887 073 291.

4 Which monitors show a number that has

(a) a thousands digit greater than 5

(b) a hundreds of millions digit less than 8

(c) a millions digit less than 4

(d) a tens of thousands digit of 7

(e) a tens of millions digit greater than 5

(f) a hundreds of thousands digit of 8 ?

5 There is a malfunction with the crystal monitors. The readings for Week 2 are wrong. Find each correct reading. Check using a calculator.

	Week 1			**Week 2**
(a)	722 355.	→ + 10 000 →		723 355.
(b)	1 213 456.	→ − 100 000 →		1 203 456.
(c)	2 600 352.	→ + 1000 →		2 609 352.
(d)	17 906 399.	→ − 3 000 000 →		15 906 399.
(e)	86 153 705.	→ + 1 000 000 →		96 153 705.
(f)	57 007 954.	→ − 10 000 000 →		67 007 954.

6 Write the next four numbers in each sequence.

(a) 850 000, 900 000, 950 000,

(b) 3 000 100, 13 000 200, 23 000 300,

(c) 8 500 000, 9 000 000, 9 500 000,

(d) 15 588 000, 13 578 000, 11 568 000,

(e) 350 000 200, 360 000 900, 370 001 600,

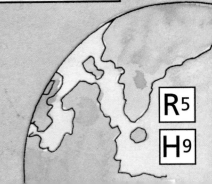

R5

H9

1 The workers on Zoid live in camps. They travel to the workzones in buggies which each carry 18 workers.
How many buggy trips are needed to carry these workers?

From \ To	Zone A	Zone B	Zone C	Zone D	Zone E
Camp Zig	216	648	1080	1530	2376
Camp Zag	162	324	1008	1098	1890

In Camp Zog there are 5675 workers and 83 droids to assist them.
To find the **average** or **mean** number of workers per droid:

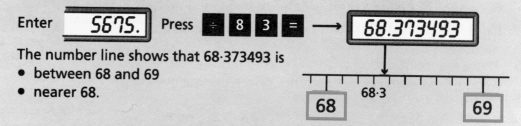

Enter `5675.` Press `÷ 8 3 =` ⟶ `68.373493`

The number line shows that 68·373493 is
• between 68 and 69
• nearer 68.

The mean number of workers per droid is 15 **to the nearest whole number.**

2 **Do Workbook page 4, question 1.**

3 For each Zone in the table, find the mean number of workers per droid, rounded to the nearest whole number.

Camp Zog	Zone A	Zone B	Zone C	Zone D
Number of workers	1225	1169	1475	1205
Number of droids	75	84	98	86

4 Use this result to answer each question. `4 6 1 ÷ 1 3 =` `35.461538`

(a) 461 energy capsules are shared equally among 13 workers.
How many capsules are given to each worker?

(b) How many water bottles each holding 13 galactolitres can be **filled** from a tank holding 461 galactolitres?

(c) Each mechanic can maintain 13 droids.
How many mechanics are **needed** to maintain 461 droids?

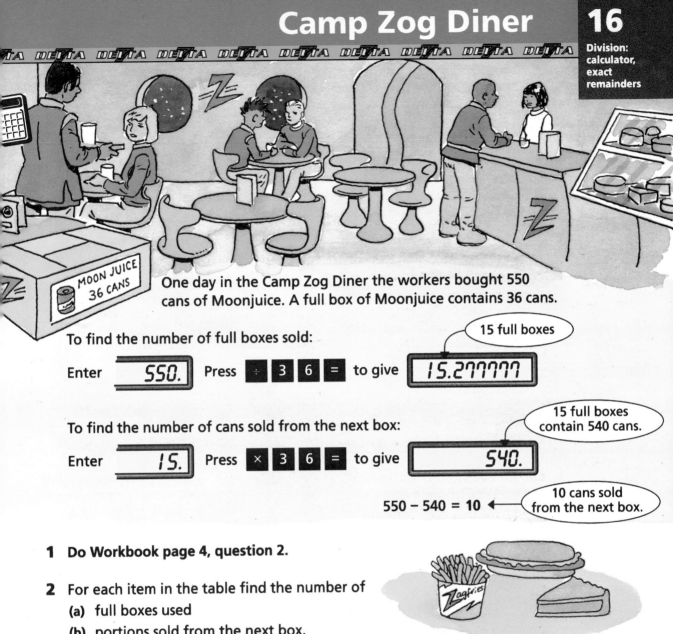

One day in the Camp Zog Diner the workers bought 550 cans of Moonjuice. A full box of Moonjuice contains 36 cans.

To find the number of full boxes sold:

Enter **550.** Press **÷ 3 6 =** to give **15.277777**

(15 full boxes)

To find the number of cans sold from the next box:

Enter **15.** Press **× 3 6 =** to give **540.**

(15 full boxes contain 540 cans.)

550 − 540 = 10 ⟵ (10 cans sold from the next box.)

1 Do Workbook page 4, question 2.

2 For each item in the table find the number of
  (a) full boxes used
  (b) portions sold from the next box.

	Zogdogs	Skypie	Moonbeans	Zagfries	Milkywayfers
Number of portions sold	580	655	967	1410	3350
Number in one full box	32	16	28	42	54

Zandra orders food from the Diner for her squad of workers.

3 Astronoodles are sold in boxes of 15 and also in single pots. How many full boxes and how many single pots should Zandra order?

4 Stoballs are sold in boxes of 12 and **cannot** be bought individually.
  (a) How many full boxes should Zandra order?
  (b) How many extra Stoballs will she have?

1135 Astronoodles
2270 Stoballs

DE**Z**TA DE**Z**TA DE**Z**TA DE**Z**TA DE**Z**TA DE**Z**TA DE**Z**TA DE**Z**TA DE**Z**TA DE

Before starting work droids test their electronic circuits.
Help Droid 492 with its tests.

1010110111100
001101010110
100101010101

**DIAGNOSTIC AND LOGICAL
ELECTRONIC CIRCUIT TESTER**

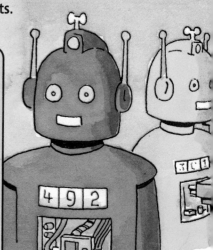

Test A

| 1626 | 873 | | 589 | 423 | | 904 | 1618 | | 2347 | 54 |

1 (a) For each microchip,
find the product of
- the two numbers
- the units digit in each number.

$$1626 \times 873 = 1419498$$
$$6 \times 3 = 18$$

(b) Look at the units digit in each **pair
of answers**. What do you notice?

(c) Do not use a calculator.
Which of these cannot be the answer to 273 × 857 ? Explain.

| 233 964 | | 233 967 | | 233 961 | | 233 963 |

Test B

$$32 + 4182 = 4510$$
4214

Check by subtracting.
4510 − 4182 = 328

4214

2 Find

(a) 2793 + 859   Check by subtracting.

(b) 2874 − 1243   Check by adding.

(c)   67 × 184   Check by dividing.

(d) 1674 ÷ 93   Check by multiplying.

Check each calculation again in a **different** way. Explain what you did.

3 Draw a logic grid like this on squared paper.

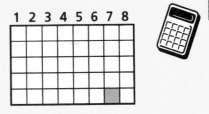

4 Multiply pairs of droid numbers. Write
   (a) the largest product in column 1
   (b) the product between 45 000 and
        50 000 in column 2
   (c) the smallest product in column 3.

171   **159**   **148**   **323**

5

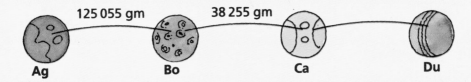

125 055 gm   38 255 gm

Ag   **Bo**   **Ca**   **Du**

The total journey distance from Ag to Du is 250 000 galactometres.
How far is it from Ca to Du?
Write your answer in column 4.

6 Transporter *Zarco*
   • weighs 144 000 galactograms
   • can carry one quarter of its weight
   • has a cargo of 3445 gg.

How many more galactograms can it carry?
Write your answer in column 5.

7

| Mining target ⟹ one million galactotonnes |
| Total so far ⟹ **909500.** galactotonnes |

What weight still needs to be mined to reach the target?
Write your answer in column 6.

8

 7603    57 063   55 324   9382   8915

Which two bogie numbers have a difference of 47 681?
Write these numbers in columns 7 and 8.

9 Colour **all** the squares in which there is a **2** **3** **4** or **5** .
What is the message on the logic grid?

R7

H12

Zarco returns . . .

**Galactometre chart No. 3A:
return distances from** *DELTA*

Planet Ag	–	1082 gm
Planet By	–	2313 gm
Planet Cob	–	1426 gm
Planet Dal	–	1107 gm
Planet Ef	–	1548 gm

1 The transporter *Zarco* makes 3 return journeys
to Planet Ag and 2 return journeys to Planet By.
What is the total distance, in galactometres, travelled by *Zarco*?

2 Do Question **1** again using the calculator's memory like this:

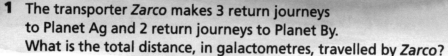

Ask your teacher how to clear the memory.

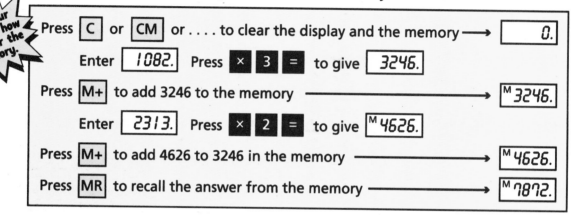

Press [C] or [CM] or . . . . to clear the display and the memory ⟶ `0.`

Enter `1082.` Press [×] [3] [=] to give `3246.`

Press [M+] to add 3246 to the memory ⟶ `ᴹ 3246.`

Enter `2313.` Press [×] [2] [=] to give `ᴹ 4626.`

Press [M+] to add 4626 to 3246 in the memory ⟶ `ᴹ 4626.`

Press [MR] to recall the answer from the memory ⟶ `ᴹ 7872.`

3 Use the memory. Find each total distance travelled by *Zarco* for these return
journeys.

(a)

3 journeys and 4 journeys

(b)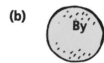

5 journeys and 7 journeys

(c)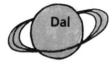

6 journeys and 12 journeys

(d)

8 journeys and 11 journeys

4 Use the memory. Find the total weight, in galactograms, of cargo in each set
of *Zarco's* holds.

Hold	Number of crates	Weight of each crate		Hold	Number of crates	Weight of each crate
Ⓐ Lineum 1	2	165 gg		Ⓑ Ambal 1	13	845 gg
Lineum 2	5	380 gg		Ambal 2	9	1020 gg
Ⓒ Rodon 1	8	224 gg		Ⓓ Zelac 1	22	463 gg
Rodon 2	17	462 gg		Zelac 2	19	1370 gg
Rodon 3	5	356 gg		Zelac 3	31	859 gg

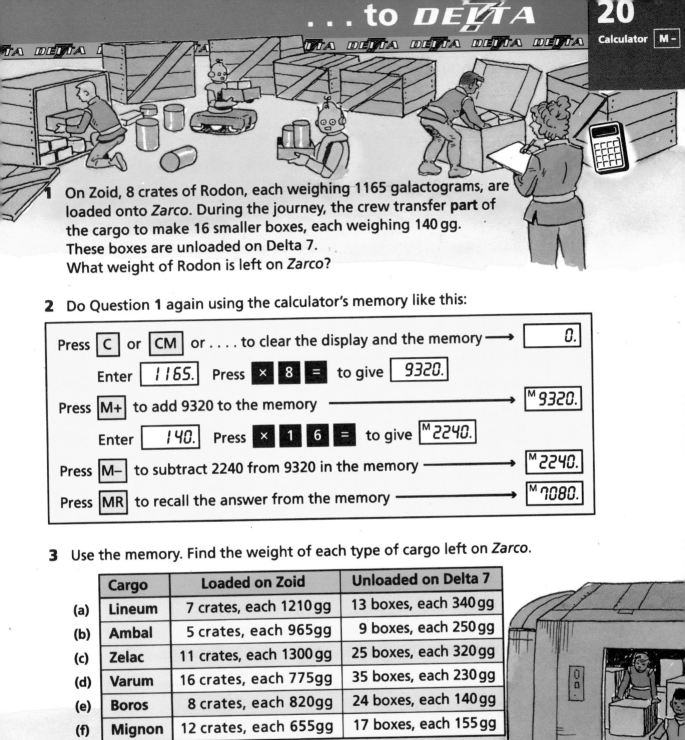

1 On Zoid, 8 crates of Rodon, each weighing 1165 galactograms, are loaded onto *Zarco*. During the journey, the crew transfer **part** of the cargo to make 16 smaller boxes, each weighing 140 gg. These boxes are unloaded on Delta 7.
What weight of Rodon is left on *Zarco*?

2 Do Question **1** again using the calculator's memory like this:

Press [C] or [CM] or . . . . to clear the display and the memory ⟶ `0.`

Enter `1165.` Press [×] [8] [=] to give `9320.`

Press [M+] to add 9320 to the memory ⟶ `M 9320.`

Enter `140.` Press [×] [1] [6] [=] to give `M 2240.`

Press [M−] to subtract 2240 from 9320 in the memory ⟶ `M 2240.`

Press [MR] to recall the answer from the memory ⟶ `M 7080.`

3 Use the memory. Find the weight of each type of cargo left on *Zarco*.

	Cargo	Loaded on Zoid	Unloaded on Delta 7
(a)	Lineum	7 crates, each 1210 gg	13 boxes, each 340 gg
(b)	Ambal	5 crates, each 965 gg	9 boxes, each 250 gg
(c)	Zelac	11 crates, each 1300 gg	25 boxes, each 320 gg
(d)	Varum	16 crates, each 775 gg	35 boxes, each 230 gg
(e)	Boros	8 crates, each 820 gg	24 boxes, each 140 gg
(f)	Mignon	12 crates, each 655 gg	17 boxes, each 155 gg

4 Some containers on the unloading buggies contain Lineum and the others contain Ambal.
The total weight of these 11 containers is 7000 galactograms.
Each container of Lineum weighs 800 gg.
Each container of Ambal weighs 500 gg.
How many containers hold
• Lineum   • Ambal?

Problem solving

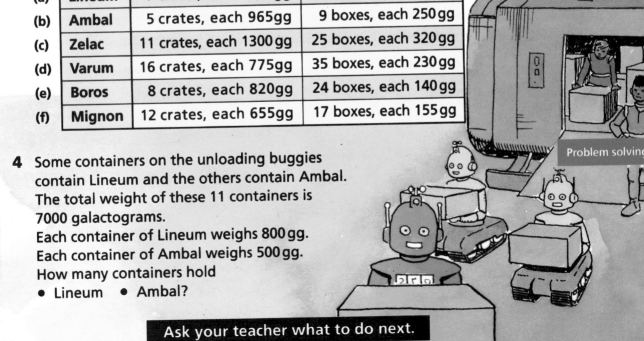

Ask your teacher what to do next.

Kitbits Company

MOSAICS SOLDIERS TRANSPORT

The Kitbits Company makes different kinds of kits.

1 Do Workbook page 5, question 1.

$$\frac{5}{8} \overset{\times 5}{\underset{\times 5}{=}} \frac{25}{40}$$

To make an equal fraction, **multiply** the top and bottom by the same number.

2 Copy and complete.

(a) $\frac{5}{8} = \frac{}{16}$ (b) $\frac{1}{5} = \frac{}{40}$ (c) $\frac{3}{10} = \frac{}{50}$

(d) $\frac{2}{3} = \frac{20}{}$ (e) $\frac{9}{10} = \frac{63}{}$ (f) $\frac{4}{5} = \frac{}{25}$

(g) $\frac{1}{2} = \frac{9}{}$ (h) $\frac{3}{4} = \frac{15}{}$

3 Do Workbook page 5, question 2.

$$\frac{28}{49} \overset{\div 7}{\underset{\div 7}{=}} \frac{4}{7}$$

To make an equal fraction, **divide** the top and bottom by the same number.

4 Copy and complete.

(a) $\frac{7}{14} = \frac{}{2}$ (b) $\frac{25}{40} = \frac{}{8}$ (c) $\frac{49}{70} = \frac{7}{}$

(d) $\frac{30}{36} = \frac{}{6}$ (e) $\frac{20}{30} = \frac{}{3}$ (f) $\frac{18}{24} = \frac{}{4}$

(g) $\frac{12}{30} = \frac{2}{}$ (h) $\frac{5}{20} = \frac{}{4}$

60 of the 80 mosaic tiles are yellow.
$\frac{60}{80}$ are yellow.
To simplify, **divide** the top and bottom by the same numbers.
$\frac{3}{4}$ are yellow.

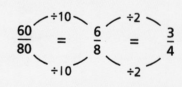

$$\frac{60}{80} \overset{\div 10}{\underset{\div 10}{=}} \frac{6}{8} \overset{\div 2}{\underset{\div 2}{=}} \frac{3}{4}$$

5 Find the missing numbers.

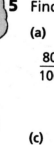

(a)
$$\frac{80}{100} \overset{\div \square}{\underset{\div \square}{=}} \frac{8}{10} \overset{\div \triangle}{\underset{\div \triangle}{=}} \frac{4}{5}$$

(b)
$$\frac{24}{36} \overset{\div \square}{\underset{\div \square}{=}} \frac{6}{9} \overset{\div \triangle}{\underset{\div \triangle}{=}} \frac{2}{3}$$

(c)
$$\frac{54}{90} \overset{\div \square}{\underset{\div \square}{=}} \frac{6}{10} \overset{\div \triangle}{\underset{\div \triangle}{=}} \frac{3}{5}$$

6 Simplify.

(a) $\frac{30}{45}$ (b) $\frac{40}{60}$ (c) $\frac{90}{120}$ (d) $\frac{40}{100}$

(e) $\frac{30}{90}$ (f) $\frac{18}{30}$ (g) $\frac{64}{80}$ (h) $\frac{63}{105}$

(i) $\frac{48}{72}$ (j) $\frac{60}{96}$ (k) $\frac{490}{560}$ (l) $\frac{200}{800}$

In the standard Misfits pack, 21 of the 42 shapes are yellow.

$\frac{21}{42} = \frac{3}{6} = \frac{1}{2}$

$\frac{1}{2}$ of the shapes are yellow.

1 Find the fraction of the shapes in each pack which are yellow.

Pack	small	medium	large	micro	maxi
Number of yellow shapes	6	4	30	8	50
Total number of shapes	18	20	45	12	100

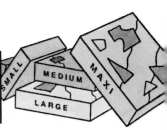

2 Find the fraction of the shapes in each bumper pack which have these colours.

(a)

red	**80**	yellow	**120**
blue	**40**	240 shapes	

(b)

purple	**60**	white	**120**
orange	**80**	pink	**100**

360 shapes

Each Circle Pack has 8 shapes. The diagram shows $3\frac{5}{8}$ packs.

   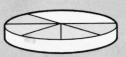

In 3 wholes there are 3 × 8 = 24 eighths.
Adding the other 5 eighths gives **29 eighths**.

$3\frac{5}{8} = \frac{29}{8}$

mixed number   improper fraction

3 Write as an **improper fraction**.

(a) $1\frac{3}{8}$ (b) $2\frac{7}{8}$ (c) $3\frac{2}{3}$ (d) $5\frac{1}{2}$ (e) $6\frac{3}{4}$ (f) $4\frac{2}{7}$ (g) $3\frac{4}{5}$

(h) $7\frac{2}{5}$ (i) $2\frac{9}{10}$ (j) $4\frac{5}{6}$ (k) $9\frac{7}{10}$ (l) $4\frac{6}{7}$ (m) $8\frac{5}{6}$ (n) $1\frac{3}{20}$

Each whole Puzzle Pack has 10 shapes. Each shape is $\frac{1}{10}$ of the pack.

26 tenths fill 26 ÷ 10 = **2 whole packs** and **6 tenths** of a pack.

$\frac{26}{10} = 2\frac{6}{10} = 2\frac{3}{5}$

4 Write as a **mixed number**.

(a) $\frac{42}{10}$ (b) $\frac{12}{8}$ (c) $\frac{14}{6}$ (d) $\frac{35}{4}$ (e) $\frac{26}{3}$ (f) $\frac{59}{8}$ (g) $\frac{33}{5}$

(h) $\frac{78}{9}$ (i) $\frac{16}{4}$ (j) $\frac{62}{8}$ (k) $\frac{21}{7}$ (l) $\frac{67}{7}$ (m) $\frac{56}{6}$ (n) $\frac{25}{20}$

R9

H14

Kitbits machines

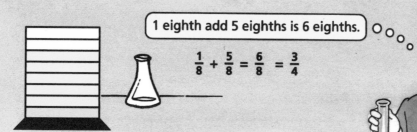

Jake mixes chemicals for the moulding machine.

> 1 eighth add 5 eighths is 6 eighths.

$$\frac{1}{8} + \frac{5}{8} = \frac{6}{8} = \frac{3}{4}$$

1 Copy and complete.

(a) $\frac{2}{5} + \frac{1}{5}$ (b) $\frac{3}{10} + \frac{6}{10}$ (c) $\frac{2}{8} + \frac{3}{8}$ (d) $\frac{1}{4} + \frac{3}{4}$ (e) $\frac{2}{6} + \frac{3}{6}$

(f) $\frac{1}{10} + \frac{7}{10}$ (g) $\frac{2}{8} + \frac{4}{8}$ (h) $\frac{2}{5} + \frac{2}{5}$ (i) $\frac{2}{10} + \frac{3}{10}$ (j) $\frac{1}{6} + \frac{3}{6}$

Mia drains $\frac{1}{6}$ of this container.

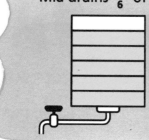

> 5 sixths take away 1 sixth is 4 sixths.

$$\frac{5}{6} - \frac{1}{6} = \frac{4}{6}$$
$$= \frac{2}{3}$$

2 Copy and complete.

(a) $\frac{9}{10} - \frac{2}{10}$ (b) $\frac{5}{6} - \frac{4}{6}$ (c) $\frac{7}{8} - \frac{2}{8}$ (d) $\frac{2}{3} - \frac{1}{3}$ (e) $\frac{7}{10} - \frac{6}{10}$

(f) $\frac{5}{8} - \frac{1}{8}$ (g) $\frac{5}{6} - \frac{1}{6}$ (h) $1 - \frac{2}{10}$ (i) $1 - \frac{6}{8}$ (j) $\frac{1}{2} - \frac{1}{4}$

The display on the plastic press shows the mixture of chemicals used.

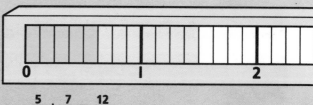

> 5 eighths add 7 eighths is 12 eighths. That is 1 whole and 4 eighths.

$$\frac{5}{8} + \frac{7}{8} = \frac{12}{8}$$
$$= 1\frac{4}{8} = 1\frac{1}{2}$$

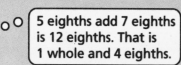

Tom

3 Copy and complete.

(a) $\frac{9}{10} + \frac{2}{10}$ (b) $\frac{5}{8} + \frac{4}{8}$ (c) $\frac{4}{5} + \frac{4}{5}$ (d) $\frac{5}{6} + \frac{2}{6}$ (e) $\frac{2}{3} + \frac{2}{3}$

(f) $\frac{8}{10} + \frac{4}{10}$ (g) $\frac{3}{8} + \frac{7}{8}$ (h) $\frac{5}{6} + \frac{3}{6}$ (i) $\frac{8}{10} + \frac{7}{10}$ (j) $\frac{3}{4} + \frac{3}{4}$

(k) $\frac{7}{8} + \frac{7}{8}$ (l) $\frac{3}{10} + \frac{8}{10}$ (m) $\frac{3}{5} + \frac{2}{5}$ (n) $\frac{4}{6} + \frac{3}{6}$ (o) $\frac{1}{2} + \frac{3}{4}$

Mia reads the display on the paint mixer. It shows the volume of each paint used.

2 wholes and 2 tenths add 4 tenths is 2 wholes and 6 tenths.

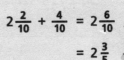

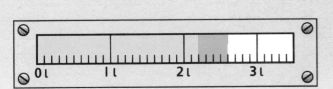

Mia

$$2\frac{2}{10} + \frac{4}{10} = 2\frac{6}{10}$$
$$= 2\frac{3}{5}$$

$2\frac{3}{5}$ l of paint are used altogether.

1 Copy and complete.

(a) $2\frac{3}{10} + \frac{6}{10}$ (b) $3\frac{1}{8} + \frac{6}{8}$ (c) $1\frac{2}{4} + \frac{2}{4}$ (d) $3\frac{1}{6} + \frac{4}{6}$ (e) $2\frac{2}{5} + \frac{2}{5}$

(f) $2\frac{2}{6} + \frac{2}{6}$ (g) $3\frac{3}{10} + \frac{5}{10}$ (h) $1\frac{3}{8} + \frac{3}{8}$ (i) $1\frac{1}{6} + \frac{2}{6}$ (j) $1\frac{1}{8} + \frac{5}{8}$

2 There is $1\frac{3}{10}$ l of paint in the spray. Jake adds another $\frac{3}{10}$ l.
How many litres of paint are in the spray?

3 Mia uses $\frac{3}{8}$ kg of powder paint and then another $2\frac{5}{8}$ kg.
How much powder paint does she use altogether?

Mia uses a different mixture of paint.

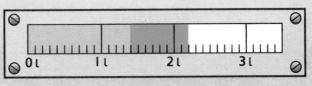

Mia

1 whole and 4 tenths add 8 tenths is 1 whole and 12 tenths. That is 2 wholes and 2 tenths.

$$1\frac{4}{10} + \frac{8}{10} = 1\frac{12}{10}$$
$$= 1 + 1\frac{2}{10}$$
$$= 2\frac{2}{10}$$
$$= 2\frac{1}{5} \qquad 2\frac{1}{5}\text{ l of paint are used.}$$

4 (a) $2\frac{5}{8} + \frac{4}{8}$ (b) $2\frac{2}{3} + \frac{2}{3}$ (c) $1\frac{7}{10} + \frac{4}{10}$ (d) $2\frac{4}{5} + \frac{4}{5}$ (e) $3\frac{5}{6} + \frac{2}{6}$

(f) $1\frac{1}{8} + \frac{5}{8}$ (g) $2\frac{3}{4} + \frac{3}{4}$ (h) $2\frac{9}{10} + \frac{7}{10}$ (i) $3\frac{5}{7} + \frac{4}{7}$ (j) $2\frac{3}{5} + \frac{4}{5}$

(k) $3\frac{1}{2} + \frac{3}{4}$ (l) $2\frac{9}{10} + \frac{3}{10}$ (m) $2\frac{2}{4} + \frac{3}{4}$ (n) $2\frac{3}{4} + \frac{1}{2}$ (o) $4\frac{2}{4} + \frac{1}{2}$

5 There is $1\frac{5}{8}$ l of paint in a tub. Another $\frac{3}{8}$ l of paint is added.
What is the total volume of paint in the tub?

6 Tom uses $2\frac{7}{10}$ m of plastic to wrap one box of kits and $\frac{7}{10}$ m to wrap another box. What length of plastic does he use altogether?

7 There is $1\frac{7}{8}$ kg of centiles in a box. Another $\frac{5}{8}$ kg is added.
What is the total weight of centiles?

The computer readings show colour levels.

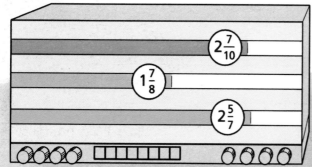
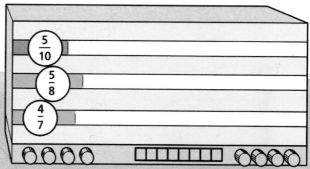

Tom subtracts to find the difference between the red levels.

2 wholes and 7 tenths take away 5 tenths is 2 wholes and 2 tenths.

$$2\frac{7}{10} - \frac{5}{10} = 2\frac{2}{10}$$
$$= 2\frac{1}{5}$$

1 Find the difference between the **(a)** blue levels **(b)** green levels.

2 Copy and complete.

(a) $2\frac{7}{8} - \frac{4}{8}$ (b) $3\frac{9}{10} - \frac{8}{10}$ (c) $4\frac{3}{4} - \frac{2}{4}$ (d) $3\frac{6}{7} - \frac{4}{7}$ (e) $2\frac{4}{5} - \frac{3}{5}$

(f) $1\frac{9}{10} - \frac{3}{10}$ (g) $2\frac{3}{4} - \frac{1}{4}$ (h) $3\frac{7}{8} - \frac{1}{8}$ (i) $1\frac{5}{6} - \frac{2}{6}$ (j) $4\frac{1}{2} - \frac{1}{4}$

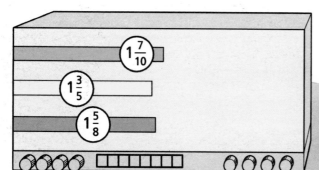
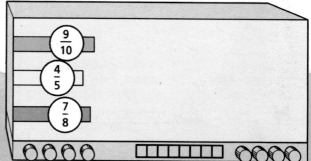

Mia subtracts to the find the difference between the brown levels.

1 whole and 7 tenths take away 9 tenths. That's 17 tenths take away 9 tenths which is 8 tenths.

$$1\frac{7}{10} - \frac{9}{10}$$
$$= \frac{17}{10} - \frac{9}{10}$$
$$= \frac{8}{10}$$
$$= \frac{4}{5}$$

3 Find the difference between the **(a)** yellow levels **(b)** purple levels.

4 Copy and complete.

(a) $1\frac{4}{8} - \frac{5}{8}$ (b) $1\frac{2}{5} - \frac{4}{5}$ (c) $1\frac{6}{10} - \frac{7}{10}$ (d) $1\frac{3}{6} - \frac{4}{6}$ (e) $1\frac{2}{7} - \frac{3}{7}$

(f) $1\frac{3}{6} - \frac{5}{6}$ (g) $1\frac{6}{10} - \frac{8}{10}$ (h) $1\frac{3}{8} - \frac{7}{8}$ (i) $1\frac{1}{2} - \frac{3}{4}$ (j) $2 - \frac{1}{2}$

R10   H15

Each worker packs one quarter of a Technokit.
Three workers pack 3 times one quarter ⟶ 3 quarters.

$$3 \times \frac{1}{4} = \frac{3}{4} \text{ of a Technokit.}$$

1 Find the total fraction of
each kit packed.

	Number of workers	Fraction packed by each worker
Clickokit	3	one fifth
Snapokit	5	one sixth
Electrokit	2	one third
Macrokit	7	one tenth

There are 8 quarters in these two Technokits.

$$8 \times \frac{1}{4} = \frac{8}{4} = 2$$

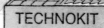

2 Find

(a) $8 \times \frac{1}{2}$ (b) $6 \times \frac{1}{3}$ (c) $10 \times \frac{1}{5}$ (d) $20 \times \frac{1}{4}$ (e) $30 \times \frac{1}{10}$ (f) $15 \times \frac{1}{3}$

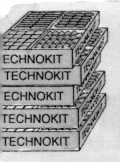

Each Technokit weighs $\frac{3}{8}$ kilograms.
The total weight of 6 kits:

$$6 \times \frac{3}{8} = \frac{18}{8} \quad \longleftarrow \quad \text{6 times 3 eighths is 18 eighths}$$

$$= 2\frac{2}{8}$$

$$= 2\frac{1}{4}$$

The total weight is $2\frac{1}{4}$ kg.

3 Find the total weight
of each batch.

	Number of kits in batch	Weight of each kit
Technokit	4	$\frac{3}{8}$ kg
Clickokit	6	$\frac{3}{4}$ kg
Snapokit	7	$\frac{2}{5}$ kg
Magnokit	5	$\frac{3}{10}$ kg

4 Find

(a) $6 \times \frac{1}{4}$ (b) $8 \times \frac{5}{6}$ (c) $9 \times \frac{1}{2}$ (d) $5 \times \frac{7}{8}$ (e) $4 \times \frac{7}{10}$ (f) $10 \times \frac{3}{5}$

5 It takes $\frac{1}{4}$ hour to pack one Technokit.
How long does it take to pack

(a) 3 kits   (b) 7 kits   (c) 12 kits   (d) 18 kits   (e) 22 kits?

H16

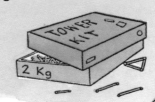

Plastic tubes make up one quarter of the weight of a Tower kit.

$\frac{1}{4}$ of 2 kg

$= \frac{1}{4}$ of 2000 g

$= 500$ g   The tubes weigh **500 g**.

1 Find

(a) $\frac{1}{4}$ of 3 kg (in grams)   (b) $\frac{1}{5}$ of 4 kg (in grams)   (c) $\frac{1}{6}$ of 3 kg (in grams)

(d) $\frac{1}{3}$ of 6 m (in centimetres)   (e) $\frac{1}{10}$ of £9 (in pence)   (f) $\frac{1}{8}$ of 2 h (in minutes)

A new machine packs some kits wrongly. Three eighths of 40 Tower kits are faulty.

To find $\frac{3}{8}$ of 40 $\longrightarrow$ $\frac{1}{8}$ of 40 = 5

$\frac{3}{8}$ of 40 = 3 × 5 = 15

15 kits are faulty.

2 Find the number of faulty kits in each batch.

	Fraction of the kits faulty	Number of kits in each batch
Tower kits	three eighths	56
Castle kits	two thirds	60
Fort kits	four fifths	45
Palace kits	seven tenths	30

3 (a) $\frac{5}{8}$ of 400   (b) $\frac{2}{5}$ of 225   (c) $\frac{2}{3}$ of 195

(d) $\frac{3}{4}$ of 2 kg (in grams)   (e) $\frac{5}{6}$ of £3 (in pence)   (f) $\frac{3}{5}$ of 2 h (in minutes)

To find $\frac{3}{7}$ of 4564,

Enter ⟨ 4564. ⟩ Press   to give ⟨ 1956. ⟩

4 (a) $\frac{3}{7}$ of 4683   (b) $\frac{7}{8}$ of 4088   (c) $\frac{5}{9}$ of 9090   (d) $\frac{3}{10}$ of 12 210   (e) $\frac{11}{20}$ of 13 440

5 There are 1800 bits in a Castle kit. $\frac{1}{8}$ of the bits are red, $\frac{5}{12}$ are blue. $\frac{5}{24}$ are yellow and the rest are white.

(a) How many bits are white?
(b) What **fraction** of the bits in the Castle kit are white?

Ask your teacher what to do next.

The *Orlando* is taking on supplies for a cruise.

This display shows that
36 hundredths or $\frac{36}{100}$ or **0·36**
of the Main Hold has cargo in it.

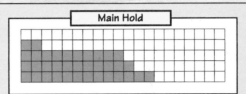

Main Hold

1 Write in **three** ways the fraction of each of these holds which contain cargo.

(a)

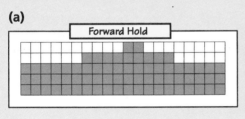

Forward Hold

(b)

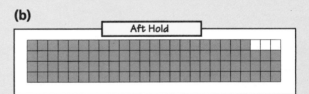

Aft Hold

(c)

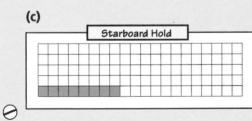

Starboard Hold

(d)

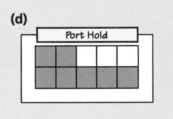

Port Hold

2 Write in decimal form:
   (a) 60 hundredths   **(b)** 9 tenths   **(c)** 6 hundredths
   (d) $\frac{19}{100}$ **(e)** $\frac{4}{100}$ **(f)** $\frac{40}{100}$ **(g)** $\frac{91}{100}$ **(h)** $\frac{1}{10}$ **(i)** $\frac{10}{100}$

3 Write in another way:
   (a) 0·55   **(b)** 0·5   **(c)** 0·05   **(d)** 0·12   **(e)** 0·2   **(f)** 0·91

4 Write in order, starting with the smallest.
   70 hundredths   0·77 $\frac{7}{100}$ 17 hundredths   1·7 $\frac{71}{100}$

5 Write the value of each red digit.
   (a) 15·42   **(b)** 3·76   **(c)** 20·19   **(d)** 4·02   **(e)** 34·95

Holidaymakers are flying out to join the *Orlando*.

On the aircraft a display shows the height shortly after take-off.

Altitude in kilometres
0·375

The aircraft's height is **375 thousandths** or $\frac{375}{1000}$ of a kilometre.

1 Write the height shown in each of these displays in **two** other ways.

(a)

Altitude in kilometres
0·816

(b)

Altitude in kilometres
0·204

1 km = 1000 m, so **one thousandth** of 1 kilometre is 1 metre.
0·001 km = 1 m, so 0·375 km = 375 m

2 Write these heights in **metres**:

(a) 0·919 km   (b) 3·276 km   (c) 10·57 km   (d) 1·015 km
(e) 0·007 km   (f) 2·5 km   (g) 4·25 km   (h) 8 km

The display shows this reading when the aircraft is flying at a height of 10 094 metres.

Altitude in kilometres
10·094

3 Write these heights in **kilometres**:

(a) 2359 m   (b) 6076 m   (c) 14 040 m   (d) 652 m
(e) 22 m   (f) 13 004 m   (g) 2000 m   (h) 5 m

4 The table shows the heights of the aircraft circling the airport.
Write the flight numbers in order, starting with the aircraft flying at the **lowest height**.

Flight No	Altitude
BA 477	5·459 km
US 242	2035 m
UK 500	0·567 km
KLM 411	6·62 km
DL 999	7·1 km
QS 343	4000 m

5 Write in order, starting with the largest number:

500 thousandths $\frac{580}{1000}$ 0·058 $\frac{85}{1000}$ 0·85

Go to Workbook page 6.

On the bridge, a display shows the *Orlando's* speed as it leaves port.

Speed in knots

5 units (5·0) → **5.367** ← 7 thousandths (0·007)

3 tenths (0·3)   6 hundredths (0·06)

1 Write the value of each arrowed digit in these displays:

(a) **4.958** ↑

(b) **0.032** ↑

(c) **17.049** ↑

(d) **31.001** ↑

(e) **9.999** ↑

(f) **102.371** ↑

2 Write the **greater** number in each pair.

(a) 0·571 or 0·057   (b) 2·122 or 2·112   (c) 0·099 or 0·105

(d) 12·099 or 12·095   (e) 3·059 or 3·5   (f) 4·01 or 4·008

3 Write in order, starting with the **smallest**.

1·405   1·45   1·5   1·054   1·045   1·540   1·504

4 Copy and complete each sequence:

(a) 1·571, 1·573, 1·575, _____ , _____ , _____ , 1·583

(b) 0·102, 0·112, 0·122, _____ , _____ , _____ , 0·162

(c) 2·375, 2·370, 2·365, _____ , _____ , _____ , 2·345

5 (a) Enter **0.326** . Add **one** number to give **0.329**

Write the number you added.

(b) Enter **0.493** . Subtract **one** number to give **0.473**

Write the number you subtracted.

6 Do each of these by adding **or** subtracting **one** number each time.

(a)	(b)	(c)	(d)
Enter **1.791**	**3.523**	**0.988**	**1.807**
↓	↓	↓	↓
Make **1.798**	**3.223**	**0.982**	**1.007**

R 11

H 18

Some of the passengers use the *Orlando's* fitness room.

1 These are distances recorded on the cycling machines.

(a) Find the total distance cycled by each person.

Cycle distances (km)

	Kay	Ann	Paul	Bert
Week 1	24·6	26·8	19·7	32·3
Week 2	19·3	28·4	26·3	25·9

(b) Find the difference between Paul's cycle distances.

2 (a) 70·3 − 31·4 **(b)** 80·0 − 16·4 **(c)** 20·3 − 6·7
  (d) 36·4 − 8·9 **(e)** 58·4 − 19·5 **(f)** 40 − 17·7

3 Find the total points scored by each person on their fitness tests.

Fitness scores

	Wilma	Zoe	Kerr	Ivan
Week 1	16·43	41·36	28·64	32·93
Week 2	25·12	33·75	36·57	28·67

4 (a) 0·69
  + 0·25

(b) 0·8
  + 0·78

(c) 6·78
  + 7·45

(d) 24·87
  + 5·9

(e) 46·7
  + 35·08

(f) 26·4 + 8·18 **(g)** 3·49 + 0·6 + 12·73 **(h)** 24·8 + 17 + 4·91

5 What is the difference between the ski-scores of

(a) Tom and Bill
(b) Tom and Jon
(c) Bill and Jon?

SKI-SCORES	
BILL	7·57
TOM	9·04
JON	8·36

6 (a) 0·97 − 0·38 **(b)** 6·04 − 3·8 **(c)** 26·8 − 12·79
  (d) 48·01 − 19·63 **(e)** 50·4 − 33·66 **(f)** 70·04 − 26·7

7 Kay's ski-score is 26·43 points. How many more points does she need to reach 50?

ORLANDO DECK SPRINT

1 (a) For each person, find the difference between the sprint times for Monday and Tuesday.

(b) On Wednesday, Mark reduced his time by a **further** 1·76 seconds. What was his sprint time on Wednesday?

Daily sprint times (s)

	Kay	Mark	Lee	Ali
Mon	34·91	40·12	36·5	38·04
Tue	38·07	34·5	33·15	41·4

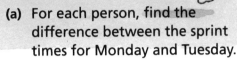

Throw the lifebelt competition! Highest total distance WINS.

2 (a) Find the total distance thrown by each team.

5·6 m 10·04 m 9·97 m

Lori's team

13·45 m 14 m 12·61 m

Fiona's team

7·18 m 14·5 m 13 m

Duncan's team

(b) Whose team won the competition? How much greater was their total distance than each of the other teams?

SEA MONSTERS

score 70 to gain 5 bonus points

3 Find each girl's score.

Problem solving

- Marnie and Hazel together scored 88·06
- The difference between Pam's and Hazel's scores is 11·14
- Pam needs to score another 31·88 to gain the 5 bonus points
- Hazel scored the smallest number of points.

R12 H19

Multiply and use the codes to find what the prize is.

Use the **units** digit from each answer to find the letter.

1 First and second words

(a) 0.6×8

(b) 3.4×6

(c) 4×1.8

(d) 2.3×7

(e) 2×8.9

(f) $6.4 \times$

units digit	0	1	2	3	4	5	6	7	8	9
letter	V	B	O	L	A	T	S	I	E	D

2 Third and fourth words

(a) 30.6×3

(b) 23.9×4

(c) 18.2×5

(d) 14.6×6

(e) 2×24.9

units digit	0	1	2	3	4	5	6	7	8	9
letter	A	T	B	I	D	O	R	H	Y	E

3 Last word

(a) 18.7×7

(b) 27.2×9

(c) 23.9×7

(d) 8×45.8

(e) 86.4×5

(f) 76.5×9

units digit	0	1	2	3	4	5	6	7	8	9
letter	B	A	G	O	R	U	D	I	E	C

4 What is the prize?

There are no passengers on Deck 2. New shelving and curtains are being fitted in the cabins.

```
┌──────────────────────────────────────────────────────────
│ │ │ │     Regal     │ │ │        │   Premier   │ │ │
│                    Plan of Deck 2                          
│ │   De luxe   │ │ │ │ │  Standard  │ │ │ │  Economy  │ │ │
└──────────────────────────────────────────────────────────
```

Each Economy cabin is fitted with 1·14 m of new shelving.
There are **7** of these cabins on Deck 2.

$$\begin{array}{r} 1{\cdot}14 \\ \times\,7 \\ \hline 7{\cdot}98 \\ \tiny 2 \end{array}$$

7·98 m of shelving are needed for the Economy cabins.

1 How many metres of shelving are needed for the
- Regal cabins — 1·22 m each
- Premier cabins — 1·17 m each
- De luxe cabins — 1·03 m each
- Standard cabins — 0·58 m each?

2 (a) 0·07 × 7   (b) 0·26 × 4   (c) 4·57 × 2   (d) 3 × 2·09
   (e) 2·78 × 3   (f) 2 × 3·98   (g) 5 × 0·68   (h) 2·47 × 4

Each De luxe cabin needs 2·64 m of curtain material.

$$\begin{array}{r} 2{\cdot}64 \\ \times\,6 \\ \hline 15{\cdot}84 \\ \tiny 3\ 2 \end{array}$$

15·84 m are needed for the De luxe cabins.

3 How many metres of curtain material are needed for the
- Regal cabins — 7·43 m each
- Standard cabins — 4·26 m each
- Premier cabins — 5·38 m each
- Economy cabins — 2·32 m each?

4 Find these lengths.
   (a) 7·53 m × 2   (b) 8·46 m × 4   (c) 3 × 6·24 m   (d) 2·46 m × 6
   (e) 9 × 5·19 m   (f) 8 × 2·09 m   (g) 3·95 m × 4   (h) 5·29 m × 7

5 (a) 26·41 × 3   (b) 18·57 × 4   (c) 2 × 47·08   (d) 5 × 16·79
   (e) 3 × 32·87   (f) 2 × 39·25   (g) 18·54 × 5   (h) 4 × 24·56

Re-stocking on Deck 4

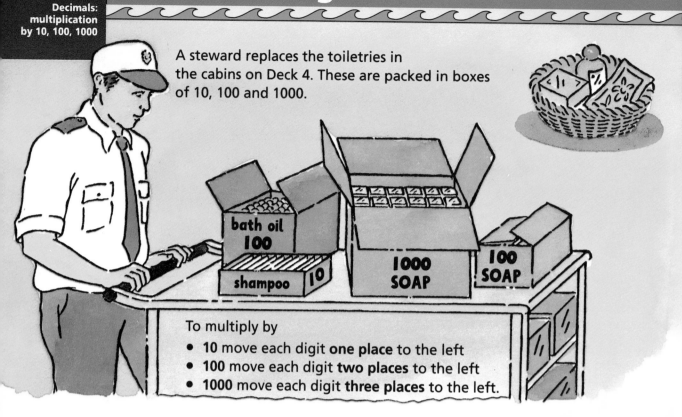

A steward replaces the toiletries in the cabins on Deck 4. These are packed in boxes of 10, 100 and 1000.

To multiply by
- **10** move each digit **one place** to the left
- **100** move each digit **two places** to the left
- **1000** move each digit **three places** to the left.

One bar of soap weighs 32·4g

10 bars weigh

32·4 × 10
= 324 g

100 bars weigh

32·4 × 100
= 3240 g

1000 bars weigh

32·4 × 1000
= 32400 g

Find mentally.

1 (a) 3·8 × 10
(e) 10 × 4·65

(b) 10 × 3·08
(f) 15·84 × 10

(c) 13·6 × 10
(g) 10 × 12·36

(d) 24·31 × 10
(h) 16·05 × 10

2 (a) 2·45 × 100
(e) 14·96 × 100

(b) 100 × 3·06
(f) 100 × 26·04

(c) 7·8 × 100
(g) 36·4 × 100

(d) 6·4 × 100
(h) 100 × 82·5

3 (a) 2·61 × 1000
(e) 3·9 × 1000

(b) 2·7 × 1000
(f) 14·8 × 1000

(c) 1000 × 24·09
(g) 1000 × 72·93

(d) 1000 × 26·73
(h) 1000 × 42·85

Bath Oil 43·25 ml

Shampoo 24·7 ml

4 Find the volume of shampoo in
(a) 10 sachets
(b) 100 sachets
(c) 1000 sachets.

5 Find the volume of bath oil in
(a) 10 bottles
(b) 100 bottles
(c) 1000 bottles.

6 (a) 43·1 × 10
(e) 8·35 × 10

(b) 8·9 × 100
(f) 100 × 6·42

(c) 1000 × 3·4
(g) 26·32 × 1000

(d) 6·91 × 1000
(h) 16·43 × 10

R13 H20

Food is to be shared **equally** among some of the *Orlando's* chefs.

1 Find how many kilograms each chef receives.
   (a) 48·6 kg of steak among 3 chefs
   (b) 7·6 kg of fish between 2 chefs
   (c) 39·9 kg of chicken among 7 chefs
   (d) 22·5 kg of pasta among 5 chefs.

2 **(a)** 4 ⟌ 31·6   **(b)** 9 ⟌ 76·5   **(c)** 6 ⟌ 69·6   **(d)** 8 ⟌ 76   **(e)** 5 ⟌ 92·5
   (f) 86·4 ÷ 9   **(g)** 95·2 ÷ 7   **(h)** 21 ÷ 6   **(i)** 98·4 ÷ 8   **(j)** 26·0 ÷ 5

3 Share equally. What weight does each chef receive?
   (a) 226·4 kg of potatoes among 8 chefs
   (b) 248·4 kg of carrots among 9 chefs
   (c) 201 kg of broccoli among 6 chefs
   (d) 144·9 kg of mushrooms among 7 chefs.

4 **(a)** 5 ⟌ 187·5   **(b)** 7 ⟌ 352·1   **(c)** 9 ⟌ 280·8   **(d)** 4 ⟌ 130
   (e) 630·7 ÷ 7   **(f)** 183 ÷ 6   **(g)** 788·4 ÷ 9   **(h)** 364 ÷ 8

5 A waiter shares 14·4 l of punch equally
   among 9 tables.
   (a) What volume of punch goes on each table?
   (b) There are 8 passengers at each table.
      What volume is allowed for each of them?

6 What volume of punch would the waiter need
   to give all the passengers at these tables 0·3 l each?

Three people shared the £8·55 prize in Monday's Draw.

How much did each win?

$$3\overline{)8\cdot{}^2 5^1 5} \rightarrow 2\cdot85$$

Each winner received **£2·85**.

1 For each day, find how much each winner received.

Orlando Daily Draw		
day	**amount**	**winners**
Tue	£8·19	3
Wed	£10·92	4
Thu	£10·01	7
Fri	£40·05	9

2 (a) $2\overline{)7\cdot34}$ (b) $9\overline{)22\cdot86}$ (c) $7\overline{)13\cdot16}$ (d) $5\overline{)11\cdot85}$

(e) $24\cdot72 \div 8$ (f) $21\cdot52 \div 4$ (g) $11\cdot01 \div 3$ (h) $48\cdot54 \div 6$

On Saturday, 4 winners shared £39. How much did each receive?

$$4\overline{)3\,9\cdot{}^3 0^2 0} \rightarrow 9\cdot75$$

Each winner received **£9·75**.

3 Share each amount equally

among 4 people → (a) £35 (b) £49 (c) £66 (d) £90

among 8 people → (e) £82 (f) £118 (g) £108 (h) £124

among 5 people → (i) £41 (j) £57 (k) £63 (l) £79

4 (a) $96\cdot85 \div 5$ (b) $75 \div 4$ (c) $66\cdot42 \div 9$ (d) $90\cdot86 \div 7$

(e) $74\cdot08 \div 8$ (f) $57\cdot30 \div 6$ (g) $95\cdot44 \div 4$ (h) $94 \div 8$

(i) $58\cdot38 \div 7$ (j) $87\cdot57 \div 9$ (k) $73 \div 5$ (l) $94\cdot38 \div 6$

FANCY DRESS COMPETITION

6·7   6·1   6·6   6·0

Jane's total score from 4 judges is 25·4
The average score for each judge can be found by dividing.

$$\begin{array}{r} 6{\cdot}35 \\ 4\overline{)25{\cdot}40} \end{array}$$

Jane's average score is **6·35**.

1 Find each person's **average** score in these competitions.

(a) Funny Face: John scored a total of 26·2 from 4 judges.

(b) Knobbly Knees: Kelly scored a total of 37·5 from 6 judges.

(c) Joke Telling: Sonia scored a total of 25·8 from 4 judges.

(d) Magic Tricks: Leon scored a total of 54 from 8 judges.

2 Find

(a) 59·97 ÷ 3   (b) 99·33 ÷ 7   (c) 142·5 ÷ 6   (d) 246 ÷ 8

(e) 117 ÷ 5   (f) 178 ÷ 8   (g) 89·22 ÷ 3   (h) 217·5 ÷ 5

(i) 188 ÷ 8   (j) 217·5 ÷ 6   (k) 88·83 ÷ 9   (l) 94·92 ÷ 7

Karaoke Competition

Total prize money £300

3 How much did each singer receive?

(a) 1st Prize £155   (b) 2nd Prize £94·50   (c) 3rd Prize £50·50

1st

Shared equally among 4.

2nd

Shared equally among 3.

3rd

Shared equally among 5.

Survival kit

LIFE RAFT

for 10 people

EMERGENCY RATIONS

12·5 litres of water
4·5 kg dried fruit
1 kg chocolate
0·5 kg biscuits

1 For each person find the ration of
   (a) water   **(b)** dried fruit   **(c)** chocolate   **(d)** biscuits.

To divide by **10**, move each digit **one place** to the right.

2 Use the rule to find
   (a) $45 \div 10$ **(b)** $173 \div 10$ **(c)** $240 \div 10$ **(d)** $18·5 \div 10$
   (e) $30·1 \div 10$ **(f)** $123·4 \div 10$ **(g)** $14·25 \div 10$ **(h)** $10·96 \div 10$

Each bandage is **425 cm** long.
To find its length in metres, divide by 100.

A calculator shows $425 \div 100$ as   `4.25`

Each bandage is **4·25 m** long.

To divide by **100**, move each digit **two places** to the right.

bandage

3 Use the rule to change these lengths to metres.
   (a) 153 cm   **(b)** 214 cm   **(c)** 333 cm   **(d)** 140 cm   **(e)** 104 cm
   (f) 27 cm   **(g)** 10 cm   **(h)** 200 cm   **(i)** 20·5 cm   **(j)** 3·7 cm

4 Find
   (a) $243 \div 100$ **(b)** $89 \div 100$ **(c)** $146·3 \div 100$ **(d)** $43·6 \div 100$
   (e) $5 \div 100$ **(f)** $7·5 \div 100$ **(g)** $30 \div 100$ **(h)** $0·1 \div 100$

5 Find the cost of **one** of each item.
   (a)   **(b)**   **(c)**   **(d)**

100 Whistles £162

10 Batteries £63

100 Salt tablets £6

100 Flares £250

Day trips from **Orlando**

SCUBA DIVING at Clam Island **£5·99**

SHOPPING in Port Minor **£9·90**

WATER-SKIING **£24·95**

CAVE VISIT **£19·98**

Diving costs £5·99. £5·99 is **about £6**.
Diving for four people costs about 4 × £6.
The total cost is **about £24**.

1 Find **mentally** the **approximate** costs of these trips.
- (a) Diving for 7 people
- (b) Water-skiing for 3
- (c) Shopping for 4
- (d) Cave Visit for 5
- (e) Shopping for 15
- (f) Diving for 20

2 Find **mentally** the **approximate** cost for each person.
- (a) *Danny:* £5·99 + £24·95
- (b) *Kate:* £19·98 + £5·99
- (c) *Farah:* £24·95 + £9·90
- (d) *Simon:* £19·98 + £24·95

3 Calculate **mentally**, **approximate** answers for
- (a) £30 − £19·98
- (b) £65 − £9·90
- (c) £50 − £5·99

4 Write each of these prices to the nearest pound.

BARBECUE **£8·35**

Dine at Minor Castle **£23·70**

CASINO NIGHT **£62·85**

CONCERT UNDER THE STARS **£16·75**

ROCK NIGHT at Club Minor **£32·40**

The total cost for the Barbecue **and** Casino is **about £8 + £63 → £71**.

5 Find **mentally** the **approximate** cost for
- (a) Concert **and** Barbecue
- (b) Rock Night **and** Concert
- (c) Casino **and** Concert
- (d) Casino **and** Dinner
- (e) Dinner, Rock Night **and** Barbecue

6 Calculate **mentally**, **approximate** answers for
- (a) £100 − £62·80
- (b) £20 − £15·30
- (c) £50 − £24·75

1 Round to the nearest **whole number**.

    (a) 7·8   (b) 115·3   (c) 18·6   (d) 7·4   (e) 25·92   (f) 17·49

These are the depths of dives on a scuba-diving trip.

Name	Dive 1	Dive 2
Paul	36·2 m	29·7 m
Kate	11·6 m	40·2 m
Danny	25·2 m	39·3 m
Faith	32·8 m	26·9 m
Denise	19·9 m	32·3 m

2 (a) Round to the nearest metre and add **mentally** to find the **approximate** total for each diver. Record like this:

    Paul's total is about 36 + 30 ⟶ _____ metres.

    (b) Find the **exact** total for each diver.

3 For each person's dives, find

    (a) the **approximate** difference mentally

    (b) the **exact** difference using a calculator.

4 Find **mentally**, **approximate** answers for

    (a) 5·26 + 7·83   (b) 22·8 − 12·75   (c) 40 − 5·79   (d) 4·25 + 38·2

    (e) 8·9 + 105·2   (f) 100 − 34·25   (g) 10·81 − 6·7   (h) 112·8 + 9·6

These are times, in seconds, for two water-ski runs.

    Danny: 42·7 + 36·0   Farah: 48·3 + 31·1

    Simon: 56·7 + 49·9   Kay: 69·8 + 66·4

    Anne: 37·4 + 50·7   Paul: 73·3 + 49·8

5 (a) Find **mentally** an **approximate** total time for each skier.

    (b) Who have total times of more than 2 minutes?

    (c) Use a calculator to find **exact** totals for each person.

6 Calculate **mentally** to find who had the **greatest difference** between their two times. Check with a calculator.

Go to Workbook page 7.

R15 H22

ENTRANCE CHARGES

Adult ....£12·63
Child ....£6·23

EXTRA CHARGES
Boat, per person   85p
Guide for group   £9·50

1 Find the total cost for each of these groups visiting the caves.

(a) 24 adults, entering on foot

(b) 18 children, on foot, with a guide

(c) 4 adults and 7 children, on foot

(d) 6 adults and 12 children, entering on foot, with a guide

(e) 5 adults and 27 children, entering by boat.

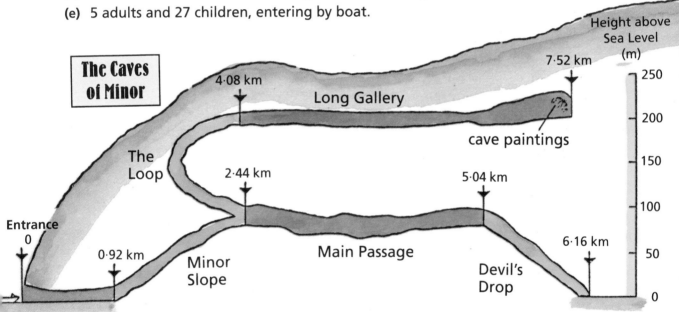

The markers ⊤ show distances, in kilometres, **from the Entrance**.

2 Find the length of each of these passages.

(a) Minor Slope   (b) The Loop   (c) Main Passage

3 Find the distance for each of these journeys.

(a) From the foot of Minor Slope to the top of Devil's Drop

(b) A **return** journey from the entrance to the cave paintings

(c) From the top of Devil's Drop to the start of Long Gallery

4 Describe where these people are in the passages.

(a) Denise: 193·5 m above Sea Level, 6·05 km from the Entrance

(b) Paul: 62·2 m above Sea Level, 1·97 km from the Entrance.

Problem solving

H24

At Minor Castle tonight, dinner for four will cost us £23·70 × 4. That is £94·80.

1 Enter `2` `3` `·` `7` `0` `×` `4` `=`

The display should show `94.8`

Check the multiplication **by dividing**.

Press `÷` `4` `=` to give `23.7` again.

2 Multiply, and check by dividing.

(a) 48·6 × 39   (b) 72·5 × 42   (c) 7 × 119·5   (d) 15 × 70·3

3 Divide, and check by multiplying.

(a) 169·2 ÷ 36   (b) 49·3 ÷ 17   (c) 22·1 ÷ 26   (d) 57 ÷ 12

4 Add or subtract. Check by subtracting or adding.

(a) 215·3 + 47·8   (b) 66·2 + 17·89   (c) 1·2 − 0·89   (d) 17·7 − 12·85

> In the examples below, check your answers.

5 There are 625 vehicles stopped bumper-to-bumper in a traffic jam between the signs for ⟨ 6 km ⟩ and ⟨ 3 km ⟩ to Port Minor.

Find (a) the distance, in **metres**, between the two signs

     (b) the average length taken by a vehicle in this jam.

6 These are the bus company's costs for the 78 km return trip from Port Minor to the Caves.

Petrol: 28 litres at 57·5p per litre	
Tax and insurance: £1·67 per kilometre	
Driver's wages: £48·35	Tour guide's fee: £35·20

(a) Calculate the costs for • petrol • tax and insurance.

(b) What are the company's **total** costs?

(c) There are 15 passengers on the trip, each paying £19·98. How much is this altogether?

(d) How much profit does the bus company make?

211·6 litres of punch is poured into bowls, each holding 8 litres.

(a) How many bowls are needed?

(b) How many **full** bowls are there?

211·6 ÷ 8 = | 26.45 |

27 bowls are needed. **26** bowls are full.

1 Jugs which hold 3 litres are used for 49·5 litres of Orlando Fizz.

(a) How many jugs are needed?

(b) How many **full** jugs are there?

2 How many kebabs can be made from

(a) 3050 pieces of meat with 8 pieces on each kebab

(b) 1665 pieces of fish with 6 pieces on each kebab

(c) 4186 pieces of fruit with 16 pieces on each kebab?

3 Twleve passengers can be seated at each table. How many tables are needed for

(a) 177 passengers   (b) 270 passengers

(c) 441 passengers   (d) 519 passengers?

4 A box of 300 balloons is shared equally among 24 tables. How many balloons are there for each table?

5 Each box has 15 candles. How many boxes have to be opened to give the 189 candles needed for the tables?

Candles

6 How many 85 g burgers can the chefs make from 965·6 g of burger mixture?

Ask your teacher what to do next.

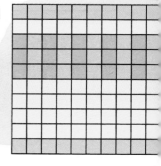

In each Centile kit, 100 congruent coloured tiles are used to make a design.

In this design 35 of the 100 tiles are blue.

35 out of 100 = $\frac{35}{100}$ = 35%

35% of the design is blue.

1 For each design, find the percentage coloured
   • red   • blue   • yellow.

(a)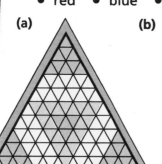

(b)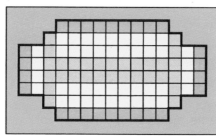

(c)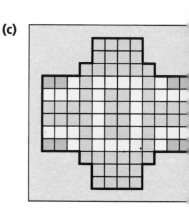

2 **Do Workbook page 9, question 1.**

3 32% of this design is complete.
   What percentage is **not** complete?

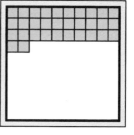

4 For each design, find the percentage
   • complete   • not complete.

(a)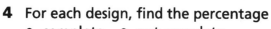

(b)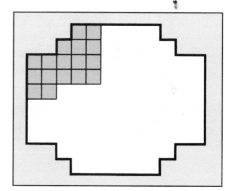

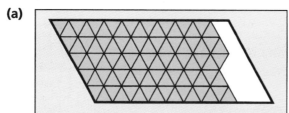

5 **(a)** The Chinese Centile kit uses only blue and white tiles.
       65% of the tiles are blue. What percentage are white?

   (b) 25% of the kits sold have small tiles, 37% have large tiles and the rest
       have medium tiles. What percentage have medium tiles?

SMALL
MEDIUM
LARGE

6 **Do Workbook page 9, questions 2 and 3.**

The Kitbits Company makes
sets of model soldiers.

40% of the Hussars carry lances.

$$40\% = \frac{40}{100} = \frac{4}{10} = \frac{2}{5}$$ $\frac{2}{5}$ of the Hussars carry lances.

1 Write as a fraction in simplest form:

    (a) 70%   **(b)** 15%   **(c)** 4%   **(d)** 60%   **(e)** 24%   **(f)** 65%

$50\% = \frac{1}{2}$	$25\% = \frac{1}{4}$	$10\% = \frac{1}{10}$	$1\% = \frac{1}{100}$	$75\% = \frac{3}{4}$

There are 200 soldiers in the Mediaeval kit.

1% of 200

$= \frac{1}{100}$ of 200

$= 2$

> 50% carry long bows
> 10% carry swords
> 25% carry pikes
> 1% carry daggers

2 soldiers carry daggers.

2 How many soldiers carry   **(a)** longbows   **(b)** swords   **(c)** pikes?

3 Find

    (a) 50% of 20   **(b)** 25% of 36   **(c)** 50% of 18   **(d)** 10% of 90

    (e) 25% of 84   **(f)** 1% of 300   **(g)** 10% of 650   **(h)** 25% of 64

    (i) 10% of 150   **(j)** 1% of 900   **(k)** 75% of 40   **(l)** 75% of 28

4 In the Roman kit, 10% of the soldiers
ride horses and 75% have swords.

    How many soldiers   **(a)** ride horses   **(b)** have swords?

5 The number of soldier kits made in November
was 9420 and in December was 3560.
In each month,
- 50% were Roman
- 10% were Mediaeval
- 25% were Hussars.

    (a) How many of each type of kit were made in • November • December?
    (b) Why do you think more kits were made in November than in December?

H26

30% of the 650 balloon kits made last week were red. 30% is 3 times 10%.

10% of 650 = 65
30% of 650 = 3 × 65 = 195
195 red balloon kits were made.

1 Find (a) 30% of 210 (b) 40% of 380 (c) 90% of 130 (d) 70% of 450

2 On Monday, 4850 car kits were made.
- 40% were sports cars
- 30% were racing cars
- 20% were classic cars

and the rest were vintage cars.
How many of each type were made?

15% of the 140 ship kits made last week were wooden. 15% is 10% and 5%.

10% of 140 = 14
 5% of 140 = 7
15% of 140 = 21
21 wooden kits were made.

3 Find (a) 15% of 260 (b) 15% of 620 (c) 15% of 580 (d) 15% of 7400

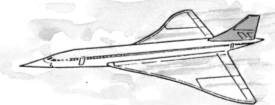

4 On Tuesday, 8600 aeroplane kits were made. 15% of these were Concordes. How many Concorde kits were made?

Problem solving

5 Find the number of tram cars sold.

9800 made, 35% sold

6 On Wednesday, 9500 transport kits were made.
60% of these were buses.
15% of the buses were faulty.
How many buses were faulty?

$14\% = \frac{14}{100} = 0.14$

Maureen is sending 14% of the jigsaws in stock to Kemp's Supermarket.
She writes 14% as a decimal like this:

$$14\% = \frac{14}{100} = 0.14$$

1 Change to decimals:

(a) 16% (b) 97% (c) 45% (d) 26%
(e) 40% (f) 70% (g) 7%   (h) 4%
(i) 21% (j) 1%   (k) 10% (l) 100%

There are 350 jigsaws in stock. Maureen calculates 14% of 350:

49.

Enter `0.14` Press `×` `3` `5` `0` `=` to give `49.`

She sends **49 jigsaws** to Kemp's.

2 Find the number of each of these items sent to Kemp's.

(a)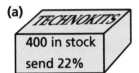
TECHNOKITS
400 in stock
send 22%

(b)
ELECTROKITS
250 in stock
send 16%

(c)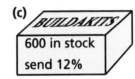
BUILDAKITS
600 in stock
send 12%

(d)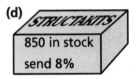
STRUCTAKITS
850 in stock
send 8%

3 Find (a) 32% of 225   (b) 15% of 320   (c) 18% of 350   (d) 7% of 1800

4 Find, **to the nearest whole number:**

(a) 24% of 420   (b) 18% of 776   (c) 9% of 835   (d) 4% of 1310
(e) 13% of 460   (f) 17% of 645   (g) 30% of 275   (h) 3% of 1690

5 (a) More of these kits are to be made. Find how many **more.**

Kit	Number made now	Increase in kits
Mosaic	4200	14% more
Buildakit	3150	6% more
Technokit	2880	55% more

(b) Fewer of these kits are to be made. Find how many **fewer.**

Kit	Number made now	Decrease in kits
Vintage car	3900	11% fewer
Galleon	6450	4% fewer
Balloon	2750	28% fewer

Kitbits News

PRODUCTION TARGETS TO CHANGE

ORDERS

Parkland School Technokits required	
age group	number
3 to 5 years	36
6 to 8 years	24
older than 8	40
total	100

Queensway School Jigsaws required	
age group	number
3 to 5 years	29
6 to 8 years	33
older than 8	38
total	100

Crinan School Buildakits required	
age group	number
3 to 5 years	42
6 to 8 years	24
older than 8	34
total	100

1 Write the number of kits for each age group as a **fraction** and as a **percentage** of each school's total order.

Newton Centre Jigsaws required	
size	number
large	17
small	8
total	25

Newton Centre ordered 17 large jigsaws out of a total of 25.

$$\frac{17}{25} = \frac{68}{100} = 68\% \qquad \textbf{68\% were large.}$$

2 Write the number of small jigsaws as a fraction and as a percentage of the total order.

3 Repeat question 2 for these orders.

Jigsaws

Order	(a)	(b)	(c)	(d)	(e)	(f)
Small	6	34	29	13	8	11
Total	25	50	50	20	20	25

Redlands Group Constructakits required	
size	number
large	18
small	6
total	24

Redlands Group ordered 18 large Constructakits out of a total of 24.

$$\frac{18}{24} = \frac{3}{4} = \frac{75}{100} = 75\% \qquad \textbf{75\% were large.}$$

4 Write the number of small Constructakits as a fraction and as a percentage of the total order.

5 Write as a percentage of each order the number of
- large kits
- small kits   *Constructakits*

Order	(a)	(b)	(c)	(d)	(e)	(f)
Large	8	16	3	23	21	4
Small	24	16	27	23	7	36

R19

H29

6 Write as a percentage:

(a) $\frac{5}{10}$ (b) $\frac{7}{25}$ (c) $\frac{6}{12}$ (d) $\frac{9}{20}$ (e) $\frac{18}{50}$ (f) $\frac{41}{100}$ (g) $\frac{4}{16}$

Problem solving

7 Lome Centre ordered 30 large Buildakits. This was 25% of their total order. Small Buildakits made up the rest of the order. How many of these were ordered?

CODE

5%	→	I	0·06	→	W	10%	→	H	$\frac{7}{50}$	→	C
0·15	→	N	$\frac{21}{100}$	→	D	0·22	→	T	$\frac{6}{25}$	→	Y
0·42	→	U	$\frac{1}{2}$	→	K	$\frac{3}{4}$	→	A	0·8	→	O

Win a Spykit, Technokit or Mystery kit

1 **(a)** Decode the message. You will have to think of each fraction in another way.

Message

| 6% | $\frac{1}{10}$ | $\frac{5}{100}$ | 14% | 0·1 | | 50% | $\frac{1}{20}$ | 22% | | 0·21 | 80% |

| 24% | $\frac{4}{5}$ | 42% | | $\frac{6}{100}$ | 0·75 | 15% | $\frac{11}{50}$ | | $\frac{22}{100}$ | $\frac{8}{10}$ | $\frac{3}{50}$ | 0·05 | $\frac{3}{20}$ |

(b) Reply to the message but **not** in code.

2 Of the people who entered the competition, 0·4 were girls, $\frac{9}{20}$ were boys and the rest were adults.

(a) Did more boys or girls enter?

(b) What percentage of entrants were adults?

3 The table shows the fraction of all the winners who chose each kit as a prize.

Kit chosen	Week 1	Week 2	Week 3	Week 4	Week 5	Week 6
Spykit	0·04	0·07	0·11	0·19	0·28	0·36
Technokit	$\frac{7}{25}$	$\frac{6}{20}$	$\frac{1}{4}$	$\frac{11}{50}$	$\frac{2}{10}$	$\frac{4}{25}$
Mystery kit	68%					

(a) Copy and complete the table writing **every** fraction as a percentage.

(b) In which weeks did more winners choose Spykits than Technokits?

(c) In which week was the total number of Technokits and Spykits chosen greater than the Mystery kits?

4 There were 2000 winners altogether.
One half of the winners lived in England,
10% lived in Northern Ireland,
one quarter of the **remaining** winners lived in Wales
and the rest in Scotland.

(a) What **percentage** of the winners lived in Wales?

(b) **How many** winners lived in Scotland?

Problem solving

R20 H30

1 Sam asked his classmates which kit each would buy.

(a) How many classmates did he ask?

(b) What fraction of his classmates would buy

- a Technokit
- a Spykit
- a Dinosaurkit
- a Mystery kit?

Which kit would you buy?

Technokit	‖‖‖ ‖‖
Spykit	‖‖‖ ‖‖‖ ‖
Dinosaurkit	‖‖‖ ‖‖‖ ‖
Mystery kit	‖‖‖

Sam finds the **percentage** who would buy a Technokit. 8 out of 31 chose a Technokit.

Enter ⎢ 8. ⎢ Press ⎢÷⎢ ⎢3⎢ ⎢1⎢ ⎢=⎢ to give ⎢ 0.2580645 ⎢

25 hundredths

That's 25·80645% which is 26% to the nearest whole number.

2 Find, **to the nearest whole number**, the percentage of Sam's classmates who would buy a (a) Spykit (b) Dinosaurkit (c) Mystery kit.

3 Find each fraction as a percentage.

(a) $\frac{13}{30}$ (b) $\frac{17}{29}$ (c) $\frac{25}{41}$ (d) $\frac{14}{35}$ (e) $\frac{32}{47}$ (f) $\frac{43}{52}$ (g) $\frac{3}{54}$

4 Leanne carried out a survey to find how much parents would pay for a Spykit.

Spending on Spykits

Less than £4
£4 to £5·99
£6 to £7·99
£8 to £9·99
£10 or more

0 2 4 6 8 10 12
Number of parents

(a) How many parents did she ask?

(b) What **fraction** of the parents would pay

- less than £4
- £4 to £5·99
- £6 to £7·99
- £8 to £9·99
- £10 or more?

(c) What **percentage** of parents would pay each amount?

New Super Spykit

5 (a) Carry out a survey to find which one of these items your classmates would choose to put in the new Super Spykit.

(b) Find the number of classmates choosing each item as a percentage of the total surveyed.

Ask your teacher what to do next.

decoder | walkie talkie | mini camera | micro-bug | binoculars

Research GLOBAL Technology

1 Dr. Zelman's monitors show cosmic frequencies.
Copy and complete the pattern in each row.

(a)

| 3 | 12 | 21 | 30 | | |

(b)

| 150 | 125 | 100 | | 50 | |

(c)

| 4 | 8 | 16 | 32 | | |

(d)

| 7 | 21 | 35 | | 63 | |

(e)

| | | 345 | 456 | 567 | 678 |

(f)

| 69 | 56 | 43 | | | |

2 Write the **first six** numbers in each of these sequences.

(a)
Start with 10 and add on 21 each time.

(b)
Start with 160 and halve the number each time.

(c)
Start with 4.
Add 1, then add 2, then add 3, then add 4 . . .

(d)
Start with 100.
Subtract 1, then subtract 3, then subtract 5 . . . and so on . . .

Go to Workbook page 10.

H31

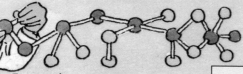

Anton is making scientific models using coloured beads.

1 For each pattern,
- make a table like this ➝

Number of red beads	Number of yellow beads

- write a rule to find the number of yellow beads when you know the number of red beads
- find the number of yellow beads when there are 10 red beads.

(a)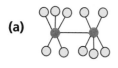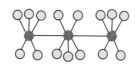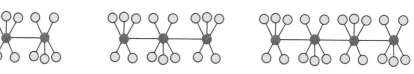

(b)

(c)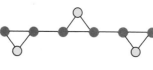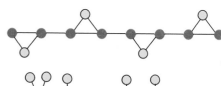

(d)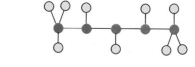

2 (a) Make a table for this pattern.

Number of blue beads	Number of green beads

(b) Write a rule to find the number of green beads when you know the number of blue beads.

(c) Find the number of green beads when there are
- 8 • 15 • 25 • 40 blue beads.

3 For each pattern, write a rule to find the number of red beads and find the missing numbers.

(a)

White beads	Red beads
2	8
5	11
7	13
24	■

(b)

White beads	Red beads
10	6
8	4
5	1
16	■

(c)

White beads	Red beads
70	10
49	7
14	2
56	■

Clare is experimenting with liquid plant foods.
The label on *Wondergrow* reads as follows:

* Fill the can with water.
* Add 2 drops of *Wondergrow*
  for each litre of water.

1 Copy and complete

(a) the table for adding drops of *Wondergrow*

(b) this rule: the number of drops

is _____ times the number of litres.

Number of litres	Number of drops
1	→ 2
2	→
3	
4	
5	
6	

This rule can be written as a **formula** like this:
D = 2 x L
where **D** is the number of drops of *Wondergrow*
and **L** is the number of litres of water.

2 For each of these plant foods,

(a) make a table

(b) write a rule, in words, for finding the number of drops

(c) write a formula for **D**, the number of drops,
which uses **L**, the number of litres of water.

Boost

Add 4 drops to
each litre of water.

Green fingers

Add one drop for each
litre of water and then
add 3 more drops.

Zoom

Add 3 drops
per litre of water.

3 For each table,
write a formula
for **D**, using **L**.

D = [____]

(a)
L	D
2	→ 1
3	→ 2
4	→ 3
5	→ 4

(b)
L	D
1	→ 4
2	→ 5
3	→ 6
4	→ 7

(c)
L	D
5	→ 1
10	→ 2
15	→ 3
20	→ 4

4 Clare uses microchips to make a growth detector.
Each microchip has 6 metal tags. ⟶

(a) Find the number of tags on • 4 microchips • 8 microchips.

(b) Write a rule, in words, for finding the number of tags.

(c) Write a formula for **T**, the number of tags, **T =** [____]
using **M** for the number of microchips.

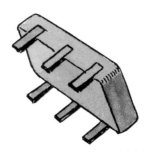

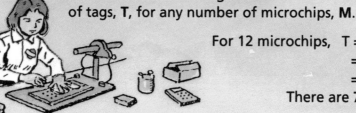

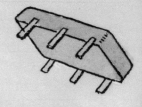

The formula **T = 6 x M** gives the total number of tags, **T**, for any number of microchips, **M**.

For 12 microchips, T = 6 × M
= 6 × 12
= 72
There are **72 tags**.

1 Use the formula **T = 6 × M** to find the total number of tags for
(a) 5 microchips (b) 10 microchips (c) 20 microchips.

2 The microchips in Clare's growth detector cost £1 each.
They fit onto one circuit board, costing £2.

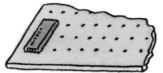

1 microchip

2 microchips

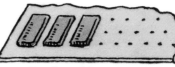

3 microchips

(a) Copy and complete the table to show the cost when Clare uses 1, 2, 3, . . . 6 microchips.
(b) Which formula is correct?
    C = 2 × M   C = M – 2   C = M + 2
(c) Use the formula to find the cost when Clare uses
    • 10 microchips • 12 microchips • 20 microchips.

Number of microchips (M)	Cost in £ of board + chips (C)
1	3
2	
3	

3 (a) Find the number of holes in each circuit board.

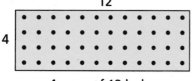

12
4
4 rows of 12 holes

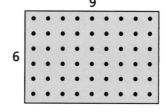

9
6

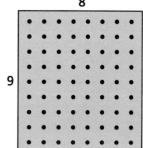

8
9

(b) The 6 tags on each microchip fit into the holes in the circuit boards.
How many microchips can fit into each of these boards?
(c) Write a formula for **M**, the number of microchips, which can fit into a board with **H** holes.
(d) Use your formula to find **M** when
    • H = 36 • H = 60 • H = 120.

R21 H33

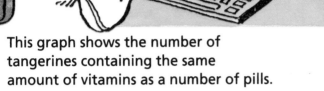

1 This graph shows the number of
tangerines containing the same
amount of vitamins as a number of pills.

(a) Use the graph. Copy and complete
this table.

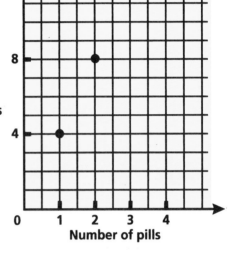

Tangerine vitamin pills

Number of pills (P)	Number of tangerines (T)
1	→
2	
3	
4	

(b) Write a formula for T. | T = |

(c) Use the formula to find the number of tangerines with the same amount
of vitamins as • 8 pills • 10 pills • 13 pills • 25 pills.

2 This graph shows the number of lemons
containing the same amount of
vitamins as a number of capsules.

(a) Copy and complete this table.

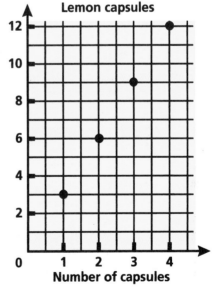

Lemon capsules

Number of capsules (C)	Number of lemons (L)
1	→
2	
3	
4	

(b) Write a formula for L. | L = |

(c) Use the formula to find the number of lemons with the same amount
of vitamins as • 6 capsules • 14 capsules • 21 capsules • 40 capsules.

Go to Workbook page 12.

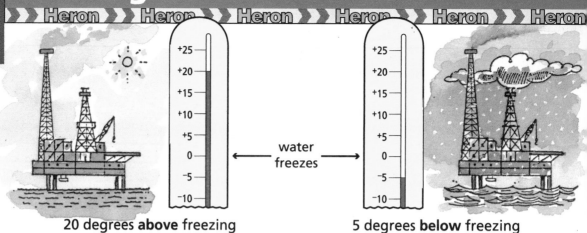

20 degrees **above** freezing
or **positive** 20° Celsius *or* ⁺20°C

5 degrees **below** freezing
or **negative** 5° Celsius *or* ⁻5°C

1 Write each temperature in three ways.

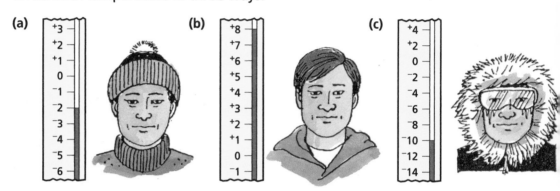

(a) (b) (c)

2 Write each temperature in two other ways.

(a) 3 degrees below freezing   (b) negative 7°C   (c) ⁺14° Celsius
(d) 18 degrees above freezing   (e) ⁻9°C   (f) negative 13°C

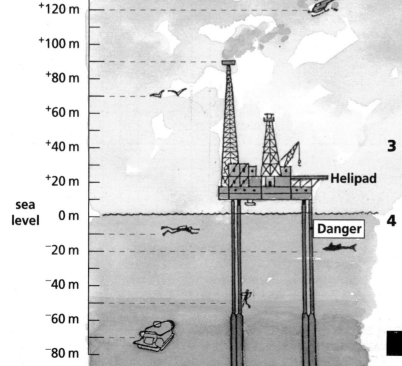

The helicopter is flying at 120 metres **above** sea level *or* ⁺120 m.

The diver is working at 50 metres **below** sea level *or* ⁻50 m.

3 Write each of the other marked heights and depths in two ways.

4 Write the approximate height or depth of
(a) the top of the crane
(b) the danger notice
(c) the helipad.

Go to Workbook page 13.

The outside temperature at Oil rig *Heron*
is recorded twice each day.

1 Find the new reading if the temperature
   (a) starts at $^+1°C$ and increases by 6 degrees
   (b) starts at $^-3°C$ and increases by 10 degrees
   (c) starts at $^-9°C$ and increases by 4 degrees.

2 By how many degrees does the temperature
   increase when it rises from
   (a) $^+2°C$ to $^+9°C$ **(b)** $^-7°C$ to $^-1°C$ **(c)** $^-5°C$ to $0°C$?

3 Find the new reading if the temperature
   (a) starts at $^+8°C$ and decreases by 5 degrees
   (b) starts at $^+2°C$ and decreases by 11 degrees
   (c) starts at $^-4°C$ and decreases by 4 degrees.

4 By how many degrees does the temperature decrease when it falls from
   (a) $^+8°C$ to $^+1°C$ **(b)** $^+6°C$ to $^-4°C$ **(c)** $^-1°C$ to $^-10°C$?

The helipad on the oil rig is heated when it has iced up.
A thermometer in the control room is
used to check the temperature of the pad.

$^-12$ $^-11$ $^-10$ $^-9$ $^-8$ $^-7$ $^-6$ $^-5$ $^-4$ $^-3$ $^-2$ $^-1$ 0 $^+1$ $^+2$ $^+3$ $^+4$ $^+5$ $^+6$ $^+7$ $^+8$ $^+9$ $^+10$ $^+11$ $^+12$

5 For each reading, give the rise in temperature needed to reach $^+2°C$.
   (a)   **(b)**   **(c)**

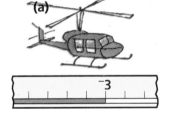
$^-3$

$^-7$

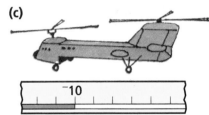
$^-10$

6 Find the new reading if the temperature starts at
   (a) $^-7°C$ and increases by 10 degrees   **(b)** $^-12°C$ and increases by 18 degrees
   (c) $^+1°C$ and decreases by 7 degrees   **(d)** $^+11°C$ and decreases by 15 degrees.

7 By how many degrees does the temperature increase **or** decrease
   when it changes from
   (a) $^-2°C$ to $^+8°C$ **(b)** $^+6°C$ to $^-5°C$ **(c)** $^-12°C$ to $^+3°C$?

Ask your teacher what to do next.

H34

SUPABOWL

> **Adults: £3·50**
> **Under 15s: £1·20**
> **Shoe hire: £1·40**

James and his mum go bowling at *Supabowl*.

£3·50 + £1·20

£3 + £1 = **£4**

50p + 20p = **70p**

Altogether it will cost us **£4·70**

£3·50 − £1·20

£3 − £1 = **£2**

50p − 20p = **30p**

It costs **£2·30** more for Mum.

❶ Find mentally the total cost for (a) Mum (b) James
of admission to Supabowl **and** shoe hire.

❷ Find mentally.

(a) £2·30 + £1·60   (b) £2·10 + £5·80   (c) £7·40 + £1·30   (d) £5·60 − £3·40

(e) £8·50 − £4·10   (f) £10·90 − £9·90   (g) £3·00 + £3·70   (h) £4·80 − £2·00

(i) £5·10 + £0·50   (j) £2·90 − £0·80   (k) £3·60 + £2·40   (l) £7·70 − £4·70

Joanne goes bowling with her four friends.

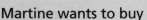
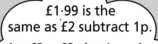

Five under 15s please.

5 × £1 = **£5**, 5 × 20p = **£1**

That will be **£6** please.

❸ Find mentally.

(a) 6 × £1·10   (b) 4 × £4·20   (c) £3·30 × 3

(d) £2·40 × 2   (e) 10 × £3·10   (f) 2 × £5·50

(g) £10·20 × 3   (h) 4 × £4·25   (i) £0·50 × 3

Martine wants to buy 4 large colas.

£1·99 is the same as £2 subtract 1p.
4 × £2 = £8, 4 × 1p = 4p.
£8 subtract 4p = **£7·96**,
so 4 large colas cost **£7·96**.

● SUPABAR PRICES ●

large burger: £2·95   large cola: £1·99

small burger: £1·90   small cola: £0·99

❹ Find mentally the cost of

(a) 5 small colas   (b) 3 large burgers

(c) 6 small burgers   (d) 10 large colas.

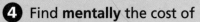

❺ Find mentally.

(a) 5 × £6·90   (b) £9·99 × 10

(c) £3·90 × 10   (d) 4 × £5·95

Quest is a computer game where you journey through a strange land to find the Golden Globe.
You must solve many puzzles on the way.

Choose two of these items.

magic dust   scissors   key   candle

1 List all the possible ways of choosing two of these items. Record like this:
   magic dust, scissors

DRAGON'S LAIR

2 To open the door
   • ring 2 different bells and
   • pull 3 different levers.

   List all the possible ways of opening the door. The order does not matter. Record like this:
   A, B, red, blue, yellow
   A, B, red, blue, green . . .

3 How many different ways can you put these instructions **in order** so that the dragon can fill his goblet?

A	B	C	D	E
Put goblet under tap	Turn tap off	Remove goblet from tap	Turn tap on	Wait until goblet is full

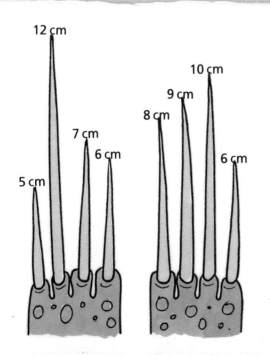

12 cm
10 cm
9 cm
8 cm
7 cm
6 cm
6 cm
5 cm

4 To continue your journey, you must use the scissors to cut one whole nail from each of the dragon's feet.
The total length of the two nails must be **at least 15 cm**. List all the different ways there are of doing this.

Put the dragon to sleep with the magic dust.
Now you must face
The Mighty Superbo.

Solve these puzzles to find how to pass The Mighty Superbo.

1 Use four **consecutive** numbers. Put them, in any order, in the red circles. Pairs of numbers must give the **totals** on the lines joining them.

33
32   34
33

2 Put three numbers, which add to 57, in the blue squares. Two of the numbers are less than 20. Pairs of numbers must **subtract** to give the numbers on the lines joining them.

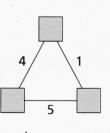

4   1
5

3 There is a number on each of these discs.

- The total of the three numbers is 46.
- The yellow number is 2 more than the blue number.
- The red number is twice the blue number.

Find the three numbers.

4 The Mighty Superbo has 57 pets.
Some are eagles, some are lions and the rest are scorpions.
There are 5 more eagles than lions.
There are 10 fewer scorpions than eagles.
How many are there of each pet?

5 Use the answers to questions 1 to 4 and the code below. Rearrange some of the letters to find what you must do to pass The Mighty Superbo.

M	I	G	H	T	Y	S	U	P	E	R	B	O
23	22	11	18	14	21	17	16	15	24	20	13	19

TO THE CASTLE OF RIDDLES

Problem solving: simulation, logical thinking

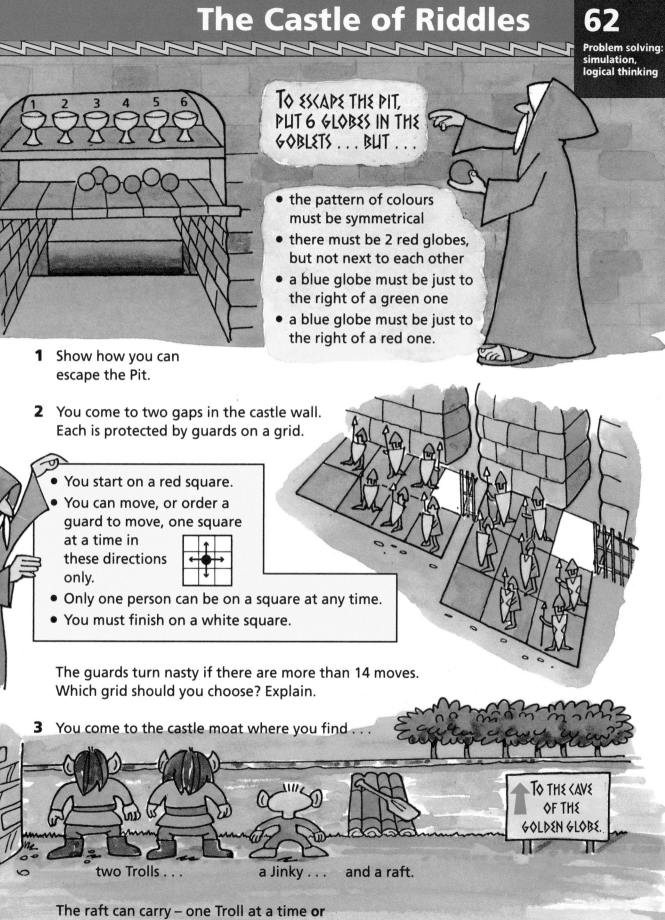

TO ESCAPE THE PIT, PUT 6 GLOBES IN THE GOBLETS ... BUT ...

- the pattern of colours must be symmetrical
- there must be 2 red globes, but not next to each other
- a blue globe must be just to the right of a green one
- a blue globe must be just to the right of a red one.

1 Show how you can escape the Pit.

2 You come to two gaps in the castle wall. Each is protected by guards on a grid.

- You start on a red square.
- You can move, or order a guard to move, one square at a time in these directions only.
- Only one person can be on a square at any time.
- You must finish on a white square.

The guards turn nasty if there are more than 14 moves. Which grid should you choose? Explain.

3 You come to the castle moat where you find ...

TO THE CAVE OF THE GOLDEN GLOBE.

two Trolls ...   a Jinky ...   and a raft.

The raft can carry – one Troll at a time **or**
       – you and/or the Jinky.
Show how all four of you can cross the moat using the raft.

Solve our puzzles and we must give you the Golden Globe.

1 Each of these pictures shows a different view of the same cube. What are the two hidden numbers?

2 Show how to remove **four** daggers each time to leave

(a) 7 small squares

(b) 6 small squares

(c) 5 small squares.

3 A total of 87 creatures live in the Cave of the Golden Globe.
They are either Goblins, Trolls or Dragons.
There are four times as many Goblins as Dragons.
There are 21 fewer Trolls than Goblins.
How many   • Goblins   • Trolls   • Dragons live in the cave?

4 Four Trolls, in a circle, pass the Golden Globe from one to the other.
The Globe must

• **start and finish** with Olaf

• be touched **once only** by each of the other Trolls.

How many different ways can the Globe be passed between the Trolls?

Josef Olaf Igor Yuri

QUEST COMPLETED

H35,36

Ask your teacher what to do next.

1 There are 34 branches of Brown's Bookshop.
An average of 85 people work in each branch.
How many people altogether work in the bookshops?

2 Multiply

(a) 14 × 56   (b) 25 × 27   (c) 43 × 60   (d) 97 × 38

(e) 90 × 54   (f) 31 × 42   (g) 80 × 70   (h) 39 × 39

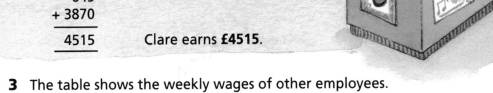

Clare works part-time in the music department.
Her weekly wage is £129.
How much does she earn in 35 weeks?

```
   129
 ×  35
──────
   645
+ 3870
──────
  4515        Clare earns £4515.
```

3 The table shows the weekly wages of other employees.

Employee	Lionel	Jillian	Ashraf	Bron
Weekly wage	£137	£241	£408	£390

How much is earned by

(a) Lionel in 13 weeks   (b) Jillian in 24 weeks

(c) Ashraf in 36 weeks   (d) Bron in 48 weeks?

4 (a) 745   (b) 861   (c) 430   (d) 209   (e) 700
        × 17   × 32   × 56   × 87   × 98

5 It costs Brown's £125 per day to advertise their Summer Sale on local radio.
What is the total cost if the advertisement is broadcast on **every** day in May?

650 books are shared equally among 27 shelves.
How many books are on each shelf?
How many are left over?

```
27 | 650
    - 270 | 10   ← 10 to each
      380
    - 270 | 10   ← 10 to each
      110
    - 108 | 4    ← 4 to each  ←  4 × 27 = 108
     2 | 24
```

1 × 27 = 27
2 × 27 = 54
3 × 27 = 81
4 × 27 = 108

books left over   books on each shelf

| 650 ÷ 27 = 24 r 2 | There are **24 books** on each shelf and **2 left over**.

1 Find how many books are on each shelf and how many are left over when
220 books are shared equally among 16 shelves.

2 (a) 12 | 392   **(b)** 21 | 465   **(c)** 840 ÷ 35   **(d)** 300 ÷ 23

Each box holds 18 books.
How many boxes can be filled from 320 books?
How many books are left over?

```
18 | 320
   - 180 | 10   ←   10 × 18 = 180
     140
    - 90 | 5    ←    5 × 18 = 90
      50
    - 36 | 2    ←    1 × 18 = 18
     14 | 17         2 × 18 = 36
```

books left over   full boxes

| 320 ÷ 18 = 17 r 14 | There are **17 full boxes** and **14 books** left over.

3 (a) How many packs of 48 bookmarks
can be filled from 880 bookmarks?

(b) How many bookmarks are left over?

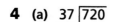

4 (a) 37 | 720   **(b)** 39 | 980   **(c)** 920 ÷ 35   **(d)** 880 ÷ 26

HEB ▵ HEB ⊘ HEB ▵ HEB ⊘ HEB ▵ HEB ⊘ HEB ▵ HEB ⊘ HEB ▵ HEB ⊘ HEB ▵ HEB ⊘ HEB

Each wallet holds 12 pencils.
How many wallets can be filled from 440 pencils?

```
12 │ 440
    − 360 │ 30   ←   10 × 12 = 120
      ───           20 × 12 = 240
       80           30 × 12 = 360
     − 60 │ 5   ←    5 × 12 =  60
      ───
       20
     − 12 │ 1
      ───
        8 │ 36
```

pencils left
over   full wallets

| **440 ÷ 12 = 36 r 8** | There are **36 full wallets** and **8 pencils** left over.

1 For each item, find how many boxes can be filled and how many items are left over.

  (a) 530 rolls   **(b)** 930 pens   **(c)** 968 glue sticks

Stickytape rolls
Box of 24

Pens
Box of 20

Glue Sticks
Box of 26

2 How many trays are needed for 928 paint blocks when each tray holds 16 blocks?

3 **(a)** 380 ÷ 13   **(b)** 750 ÷ 22   **(c)** 990 ÷ 18   **(d)** 853 ÷ 31
   (e) 835 ÷ 46   **(f)** 864 ÷ 19   **(g)** 975 ÷ 34   **(h)** 980 ÷ 27

H37

1 There are 14 computer games posters in each tube.
How many posters are in 120 tubes?

2 There are 920 Brown's Bookshop calendars to be
shared equally among the 34 branches.
How many calendars will each branch receive?
How many will be left over?

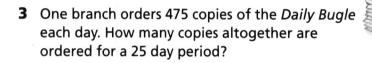

3 One branch orders 475 copies of the *Daily Bugle*
each day. How many copies altogether are
ordered for a 25 day period?

4 Each rack holds 24 compact discs.

   (a) How many racks are needed to hold 394 discs?

   (b) How many discs are in the last rack?

   (c) How many **extra** discs are needed to **fill** this rack?

**Jeremy Penrite
will autograph
copies of his
new bestseller.**

The Great Me
by
Jeremy
Penrite

You will sell 40 copies
of my book each day!

5 **(a)** If what Jeremy says is correct, how many
copies of his book will be sold in 23 days?

   (b) In fact, 980 copies of the book were sold in 28 days.
Was Jeremy correct? Explain.

6 H.E. Brown decides to give the
top salesperson in each of the
34 branches a free holiday.
Each holiday costs £199.
Find the total cost of these holidays.

Ask your teacher what to do next.

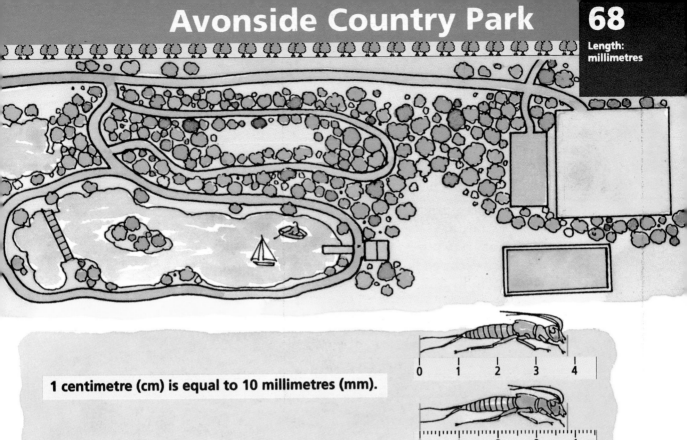

1 centimetre (cm) is equal to 10 millimetres (mm).

1 Measure, then write, the lengths of these pond creatures
- in cm and mm • in mm.

(a) Bristle Worm

(b) Stickleback

(e) Screech Beetle

(c) Newt Tadpole

(d) Blackfly Larva

2 Write in **millimetres**:
(a) 7 cm 2 mm   (b) 11 cm 1 mm   (c) 14 cm   (d) $5\frac{1}{2}$ cm   (e) 30 cm

10 mm = 1 cm	so	1 mm = 0·1 cm

3 The length of the Stonefly Nymph, 38 mm, can be written as 3·8 cm.
Write the length of each of the other pond creatures in **centimetres**.

4 Draw lines to show the length of each of these pond creatures.
(a) Minnow – about 96 mm   (b) Mayfly Nymph – about 4·3 cm
(c) Damselfly – about 3·7 cm   (d) Hydrobe Beetle – about 12 mm   68

The **scaled length** of this model boat is 4·6 cm.
The **true length** is 4·6 × 6cm
= 27·6 cm

Scale: 1 cm to 6 cm

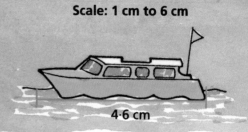

4·6 cm

1 Each boat is drawn to a different scale.
Measure each red line, then calculate the true length.

(a) 1 cm to 10 cm

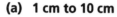

(b) 1 cm to 8 cm

(c) 1 cm to 20 cm

(d) 1 cm to 12 cm

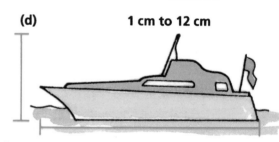

2 This sailing course is drawn to a scale of **1 cm to 150 cm**.
Find the true length of the course in **metres**.

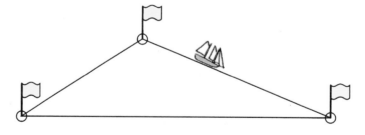

3 Find the true length of each boat in metres.

(a) 1 cm to 50 cm

(b) 1 cm to 80 cm

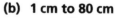

(c) 1 cm to 2 m

(d) 1 cm to 4 m

These trees grow near Avonside Sports Centre.
Each tree is drawn to a **different** scale.

Scots Pine
True height 30 m

Redwood
True height 40 m

European Larch
True height 50 m

English Yew
True height 10 m

Monkey Puzzle
True height 25 m

The park manager is making a poster to show all of
the trees drawn to the **same** scale of **1 cm to 5 m**.
He calculates the **scaled height** of the Scots Pine like this:

5 m is represented by 1 cm

5 m ⟶ 1 cm
30 m ⟶ 30 ÷ 5 = 6 cm
The scaled height is **6 cm**.

1 **(a)** Calculate the **scaled heights** of
the other trees.

(b) Design a poster like this.
Draw an accurate line for the
height of each tree.

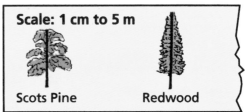

Scale: 1 cm to 5 m

Scots Pine   Redwood

2 These rough sketches show the **true sizes** of the Sports Centre's new
changing rooms.

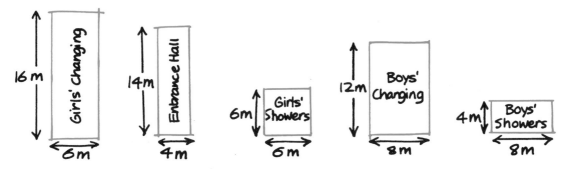

(a) Calculate the **scaled** length and breadth
of each room, using a scale of **1 cm to 2 m**.

(b) **Use centimetre squared paper.**
Make an accurate drawing of this plan
to a scale of **1 cm to 2 m.**

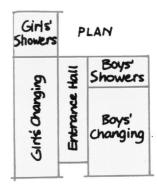

Go to Workbook page 15.

H41

A gardener is planting flowers around the **perimeter** of a **square** bed.
The perimeter **(P)** of the bed is 4 times the length **(L)** of a side.

$$P = 4 \times L \qquad \Leftarrow \boxed{\text{Formula}}$$
$$= 4 \times 2\cdot3$$
$$= 9\cdot2 \text{ m}$$

2·3 m

The perimeter of the bed is **9·2 m**

1 Calculate the perimeter of each **square** flower bed.

(a) 0·7 m

(b) $3\frac{1}{2}$ m

(c) 4 m 10 cm

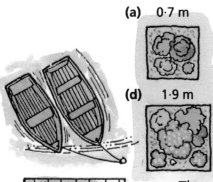

(d) 1·9 m

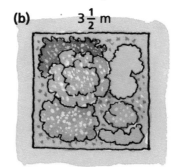

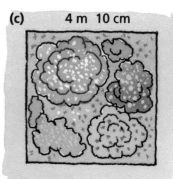

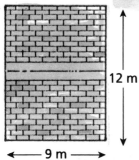

The roof of the Boathouse is a **rectangle**. Its perimeter **(P)** can be found by adding 2 times the length **(L)** to 2 times the breadth **(B)**.

$$P = 2 \times L \quad + \quad 2 \times B \qquad \Leftarrow \boxed{\text{Formula}}$$
$$= 2 \times 12 \;+\; 2 \times 9$$
$$= 24 \quad + \quad 18$$
$$= 42 \text{ m}$$

12 m

9 m

The perimeter of the roof is **42 m**

2 Calculate the perimeter of each rectangle.

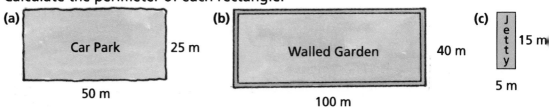

(a) Car Park — 25 m — 50 m

(b) Walled Garden — 40 m — 100 m

(c) Jetty — 15 m — 5 m

3 Measure in cm, then calculate each perimeter.

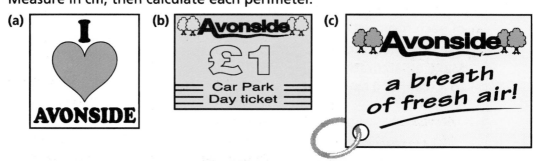

(a) I ♥ AVONSIDE

(b) Avonside £1 Car Park Day ticket

(c) Avonside a breath of fresh air!

Ask your teacher what to do next.

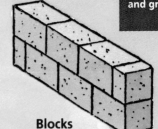

Decorative bricks

Bricks A brick weighs 1250 g = 1 kg 250 g **Blocks**

1 Write these weights in kilograms and grams.
(a) 1750 g (b) 3450 g (c) 2850 g (d) 1075 g

2 Write these weights in grams.
(a) 1 kg 320 g (b) 2 kg 405 g (c) 1 kg 20 g (d) 3 kg 5 g

A brick weighs 1·25 kg. Find the weight of 25 bricks.

 Enter `1.25` Press   = to give `31.25`

25 bricks weigh **31·25 kg**.

3 Find the weight in kilograms of
(a) 40 bricks (b) 116 bricks (c) 275 bricks (d) 430 bricks.

4 Do you weigh more or less than 50 of these bricks?

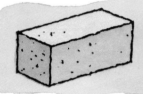 A block weighs 2·5 kg

 A decorative brick weighs 4·55 kg

5 Find the weight in kilograms of
(a) 20 blocks (b) 30 decorative bricks (c) 120 blocks
(d) 46 blocks (e) 175 decorative bricks (f) 225 blocks.

6 Find the total weight in each order.

(a)
To: P Jones
    Builder

    65 bricks
    48 blocks
    25 kg cement

(b)
To: M Ahmed
    Construction

    150 blocks
    42 decorative
        bricks
    75 kg gravel

(c)
To: L. Peters
    Building Contractor

    125 bricks
    90 blocks
    100 decorative bricks
    100 kg sand

Sand
2275 kg

1000 kg = 1 tonne

2275 kg = 2 tonnes 275 kg

1 Write these weights in tonnes and kilograms.

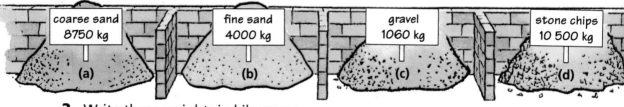

coarse sand 8750 kg	fine sand 4000 kg	gravel 1060 kg	stone chips 10 500 kg
(a)	**(b)**	**(c)**	**(d)**

2 Write these weights in kilograms.

(a) 3 tonnes   (b) 10 tonnes   (c) 4 tonnes 500 kg

(d) 25 tonnes   (e) 3 tonnes 455 kg   (f) 6 tonnes 80 kg

(g) 2 tonnes 650 kg   (h) 4 tonnes 5 kg   (i) 1 tonne 10 kg

86 bags of sand weigh 86 × 25 kg

= 2150 kg

= **2 tonnes 150 kg**

SAND 25kg

3 Find these weights in tonnes and kilograms.

(a) 220 bags   (b) 340 bags   (c) 164 bags   (d) 85 bags

CEMENT 50kg

GRAVEL 25kg

LIME 12·5kg

PLASTER 20kg

4 An empty lorry weighs 8·35 tonnes. It is loaded with 4000 bricks each weighing 4·5 kg. What is the total weight in tonnes of the lorry and the bricks?

5 Find the total weight, in tonnes and kilograms, of bricks and blocks used in these walls.

(a)

300 bricks (1·25 kg each)
80 bricks (4·5 kg each)
160 blocks (2·75 kg each)

(b)

280 bricks (1·25 kg each)
156 bricks (4·5 kg each)
340 blocks (2·75 kg each)

6 Wendy weighs 37 kg. Would 27 Wendys weigh more or less than a tonne? How much more or less?

7 A plastic centimetre cube weighs 1 gram. How many are needed to make 1 tonne of cubes?

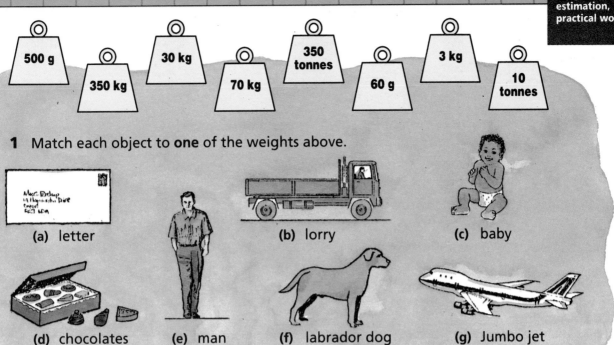

1 Match each object to **one** of the weights above.

(a) letter (b) lorry (c) baby

(d) chocolates (e) man (f) labrador dog (g) Jumbo jet

2 Choose another 4 objects and write weight labels for them.
Ask a friend to match a label to each object.

3 Which of these statements could be true?

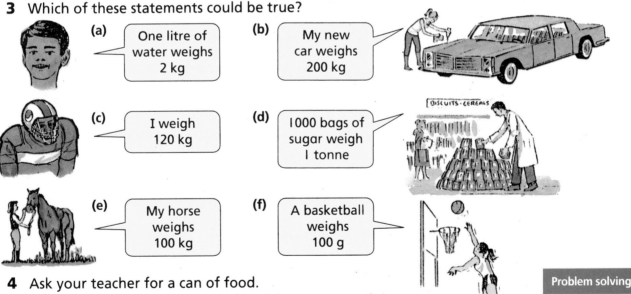

(a) One litre of water weighs 2 kg

(b) My new car weighs 200 kg

(c) I weigh 120 kg

(d) 1000 bags of sugar weigh 1 tonne

(e) My horse weighs 100 kg

(f) A basketball weighs 100 g

Problem solving

4 Ask your teacher for a can of food.
Read the label to find the weight of the **contents** of the can.
Now find the weight of the metal can without opening it.

5 Ask your teacher for
- a packet of paper
- a box of paper clips.

Find the weight of
(a) one sheet of paper (b) one paper clip.

Ask your teacher what to do next.

Creative Studio designs labels and posters for ⌈⊡⌐ music.

1 (a) How many squares are there in each row of this rectangular label?

(b) How many rows are there?

(c) What is the area of this label in square centimetres?

(d) Describe how to find the area of a rectangle without counting all the squares.

2 Copy and complete the table for each of these music labels.

Label	length in cm	breadth in cm	area in cm²
disc			
tape			
video			

For every rectangle, **Area = length × breadth**
$$A = l \times b$$

For this rectangle, $A = l \times b$
$= 6 \times 3$
$= 18 \text{ cm}^2$

6 cm

3 cm

3 Find the area of each of these rectangles.

(a) OPEN CD system
4 cm
7 cm

(b) MUSIC
3 cm
9 cm

(c)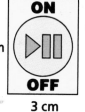
ON
OFF
4 cm
3 cm

(d) length = 10 cm, breadth = 7·5 cm

(e) length = 8 cm, breadth = 30 cm

Zak calculates the area of this transfer.

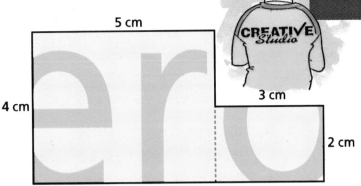

Area of
large rectangle = 5 × 4 = 20 cm²

Area of
small rectangle = 3 × 2 = 6 cm²

Area of transfer = 20 + 6 = **26 cm²**

1 Measure then calculate the area of each transfer.

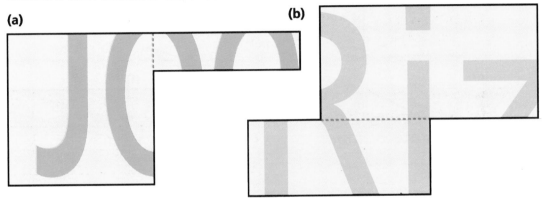

(a)

(b)

2 Sketch each diagram and calculate its area.

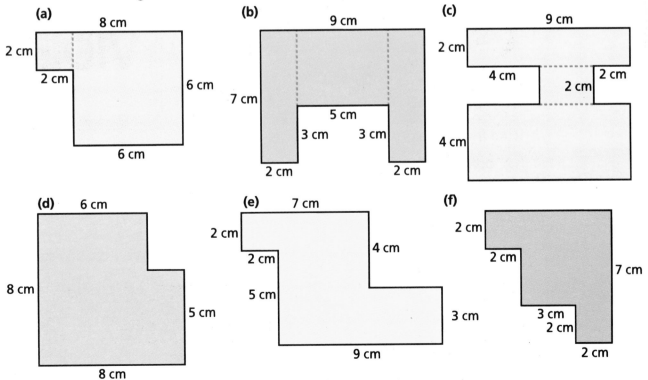

(a)

8 cm
2 cm
2 cm
6 cm
6 cm

(b)

9 cm
7 cm
5 cm
3 cm   3 cm
2 cm   2 cm

(c)

9 cm
2 cm
4 cm   2 cm
2 cm
4 cm

(d)

6 cm
8 cm
5 cm
8 cm

(e)

7 cm
2 cm
2 cm
4 cm
5 cm
9 cm

(f)

2 cm
2 cm
7 cm
3 cm
2 cm
2 cm

Area of rectangle = 5 × 2
= 10 cm²

Area of triangle = ½ of 10
= **5 cm²**

1 Find the area of each of these right-angled triangular flags and banners.

(a) GBM cars
8 cm
4 cm

(b) STOKES
7 cm
3 cm

(c) FOR TESCUE
5 cm   5 cm

(d) Dale Estate Agents
5 cm
10 cm

(e) FAX IT NOW
2 cm
9 cm

(f) Phone today
3 cm
12 cm

(g) BUY ONE TODAY
10 m
4 m

(h) DO IT NOW
7 m
4 m

(i) SALE
5 m
8 m

2 Find the total area of each of these mobiles.

(a) boat

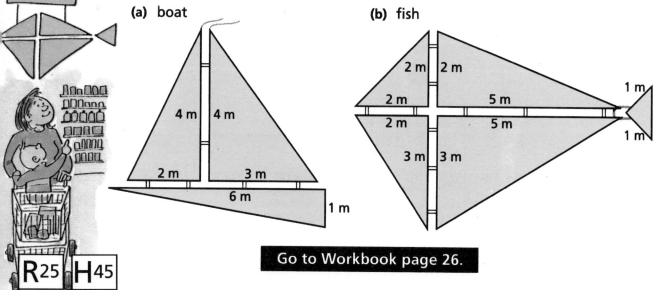

4 m   4 m
2 m   3 m
6 m
1 m

(b) fish

2 m   2 m
2 m   5 m
2 m   5 m
3 m   3 m
1 m
1 m

Work as a group.
You need a metre stick or tape, large sheets of paper,
chalk, scissors and sticky tape.

1 Make a paper square with an area of one square metre.

2 Creative Studio are building an extension.
Work in the hall or playground.
  (a) Mark out a rectangular area to represent the extension.
  (b) In your extension, mark out an area to represent
    • a rectangular rug with area 20 m²
    • a work surface with area 8 m².
  (c) Find the difference between the area of the extension
    and the area of your classroom.

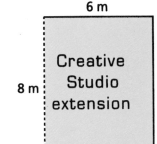

6 m

8 m   Creative Studio extension

3 A large car is about 1·7 m broad and about 4·7 m long.
Mark out a rectangle to represent the car.
What area, in square metres, do
you think would be needed as
a parking space for this car?
Explain.

Problem solving

4 Creative Studio is converting the yard into a car park.
The space for each car is to be 5 metres by 2 metres.

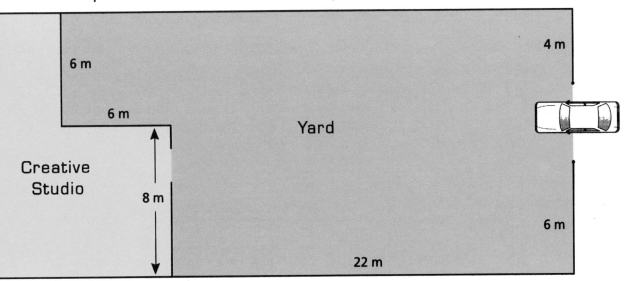

6 m

6 m

Creative Studio

8 m

Yard

4 m

6 m

22 m

  (a) Make a scale drawing of the yard on centimetre square paper using
    1 cm to represent 2 m.
  (b) Show how at least 20 parking spaces can be arranged.

Go to Workbook page 27.

Nature First produce bath cubes.
Each bath cube has a volume of 1 cm³.
This row of bath cubes has a volume
of 5 cubic centimetres or 5 cm³.

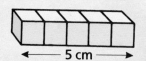

This layer has 3 rows of bath cubes.
The volume of the layer is   5 × 3
= **15 cm³**

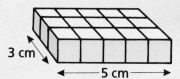

1 Find the volume, in cm³, of each of these layers of bath cubes.

(a)

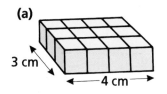

(b)

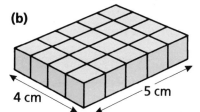

(c)

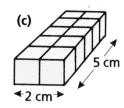

This box of bath cubes has 2 layers.

The volume of 1 layer is 5 × 3 = 15 cm³
The volume of 2 layers is 15 × 2 = **30 cm³**

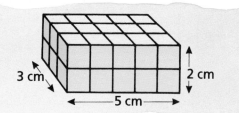

2 Find the volume, in cm³, of each of these boxes of bath cubes.

(a)

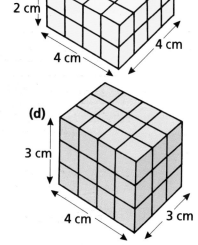

(b)

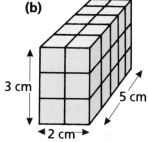

(c)

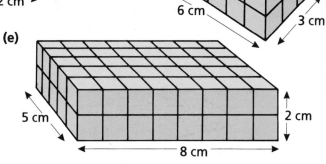

(d)

(e)

3 A cuboid has a volume of 30 cm³. How many cubes in each row
and how many rows in each layer does it have if there are
(a) 2 layers   **(b)** 3 layers   **(c)** 5 layers?

1 These cuboids are built from centimetre cubes.

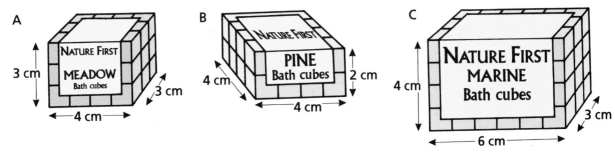

Copy and complete the table.

Cuboid	Number of cubes in a row	Number of rows	Number of layers	Volume in cm³
A	4	3	3	
B				
C				

length × breadth × height = Volume

For every cuboid, **V = l × b × h**

2 Find the volume, in cm³, of each of these cuboids.

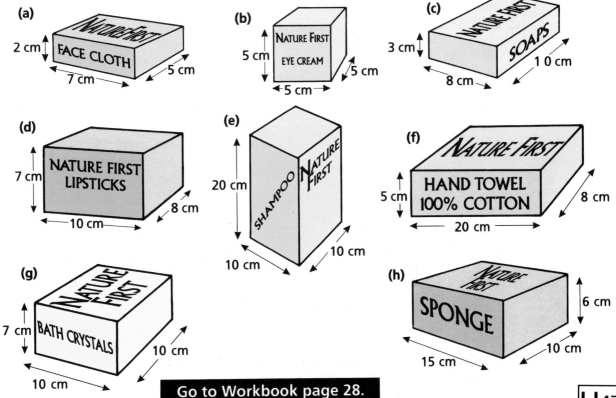

(a) FACE CLOTH — 2 cm, 7 cm, 5 cm

(b) EYE CREAM — 5 cm, 5 cm, 5 cm

(c) SOAPS — 3 cm, 8 cm, 10 cm

(d) LIPSTICKS — 7 cm, 10 cm, 8 cm

(e) SHAMPOO — 20 cm, 10 cm, 10 cm

(f) HAND TOWEL 100% COTTON — 5 cm, 20 cm, 8 cm

(g) BATH CRYSTALS — 7 cm, 10 cm, 10 cm

(h) SPONGE — 6 cm, 15 cm, 10 cm

Go to Workbook page 28.

H47

Seamaiden

SHIP MUSEUM

Join the crew of *Seamaiden* for the day!

The Martin children are finding out about life aboard an old sailing ship. They are measured, in inches, for their sea clothes.

1 inch (1 in) is about $2\frac{1}{2}$ cm

inches   1

1 **(a)** Write these measurements in centimetres.

Name	shirt (chest)	trousers (waist)	coat (length)
Paul	34 in	30 in	52 in
Lyndsay	30 in	24 in	48 in
Jamie	26 in	22 in	42 in

(b) Choose the most suitable size, in cm, for

- Paul's shirt
- Lyndsay's trousers
- Jamie's coat.

65 cm
75 cm
85 cm

56 cm
62 cm
70 cm

110 cm
120 cm
130 cm

The space allowed for a hammock is shown in the diagram.

1 foot (1 ft) is about 30 cm

$1\frac{1}{2}$ ft

2 ft

5 ft

2 **(a)** Change these sizes to centimetres.

(b) Measure, in cm, and mark the sizes in the corner of a room.
Try lying in the space. Comment.

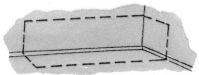

The height between decks is only 4 feet 10 inches.
4ft 10 in is about $4 \times 30\text{cm} + 10 \times 2\frac{1}{2}$ cm
= 120 cm + 25 cm
= 145 cm

3 **(a)** Find the heights of the Martin children in cm.

Paul
5 ft 4 in

Lyndsay
4 ft 6 in

Jamie
4 ft 1 in

(b) By how many centimetres does Paul have to crouch when standing between decks?

(c) Would **you** have to crouch? Explain.

The Martins help to prepare a stew for the 24 people on board.

They use 1 pound of turnips. | **1 pound (1 lb) is about $\frac{1}{2}$ kg** |

1 These are some of the other ingredients. Write each weight in kilograms.

beef 12 lb   carrots 3 lb   onions 6 lb   potatoes 2 lb

2 These are the weights of three items on board the *Seamaiden*.

cannonball 20 lb   ship's cat 10 lb   chest 56 lb

(a) Jamie weighs 30 kg. Is he heavier than 5 ship's cats? Explain.

(b) Does the chest weigh more or less than 20 kg? Explain.

(c) How many cannonballs altogether weigh about 20 kg?

The Martins help to wash up after dinner.

water 30 pints   bowl 3 pints   beaker $\frac{1}{2}$ pint   tankard 2 pints   barrel 40 gallons

pail 2 gallons

1 pint is about $\frac{1}{2}$ litre   **1 gallon is about $4\frac{1}{2}$ litres**

3 (a) Write each volume in litres.

(b) Will the full barrel of beer fill 100 tankards? Explain.

(c) The ration of fruit punch for each crew member is 4 beakers.
How many litres each is this?

(d) How many bowls of punch are needed to give all 24 crew their rations?

Ask your teacher what to do next.

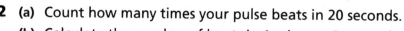

1 **(a)** Find how many times you can write this address in 1 minute. Copy and complete:

(b) Rate = _____ times per minute.

> GRT
> 42 Faraday Avenue
> Newton

2 **(a)** Count how many times your pulse beats in 20 seconds.

(b) Calculate the number of beats in 1 minute. Copy and complete:

Pulse rate = _____ beats per minute.

(c) At this rate, how many times would your pulse beat in 24 hours?

Anton makes scientific models.
He fits 240 beads in 30 minutes.
Rate = 240 ÷ 30
= **8 beads per minute**

3 Calculate these rates.

(a) signals per minute   **(b)** microchips per minute   **(c)** patterns per minute

Dr Dee sends 420 signals in 7 minutes

Clare fits 75 microchips in 15 minutes

The computer shows 3600 patterns in 10 minutes.

(d) words per minute   **(e)** pills per minute   **(f)** pence per minute

Clare types 600 words in 20 minutes

The machine makes 400 pills in 30 seconds

Dr Zelman earns £30 in 1 hour

4 At the above rates, calculate how many

(a) signals Dr Dee sends in 20 minutes

(b) microchips Clare fits in 25 minutes

(c) patterns the computer shows in 18 minutes.

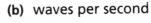

1 Calculate these rates **per second**.

(a) drops per second

(b) waves per second

(c) swings per second

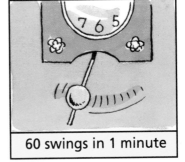

| 90 drops in 45 seconds | 70 waves in 5 seconds | 60 swings in 1 minute |

2 Calculate these rates **to the nearest whole number**.

(a) litres per second

(b) pills per second

(c) millilitres per second

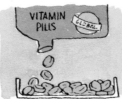

| 430 litres of fuel in 12 seconds | 144 vitamin pills in 45 seconds | 225 millilitres in 60 seconds |

3 Calculate these rates as **decimals**.

(a) sheets per second

(b) words per second

(c) spins per second

| 57 sheets in 20 seconds | 224 words in 35 seconds | 75 spins in 1 minute |

Work with a partner.

4 **(a)** Find how many tally marks (‖‖ ‖. . .) you can draw in 10 seconds. One person should draw while the other times.

(b) Calculate your rate in **marks per second**.

(c) If you could keep up this rate, how many tally marks could you draw in • 5 minutes • 1 hour?

5 **(a)** Tie a metal object (such as a key or nut) to a piece of string.

(b) How many complete swings does it make in 10 seconds?

(c) Calculate the rate in **swings per second**.

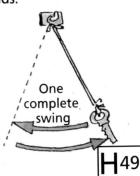

One complete swing

H49

Space vehicles

Global Research Technology is testing space vehicles.

In 10 seconds *Meteor* travels 39 metres.
In **1 second** it travels 39 ÷ 10
= 3·9 metres.
Its speed is **3·9 metres per second.**

1 Find the speed of each vehicle in metres per second.

(a) *Luna*

56 metres in
8 seconds

(b) *Comet*

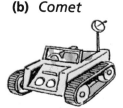

24 metres in
6 seconds

(c) *Astra*

23 metres in
5 seconds

(d) *Polaris*

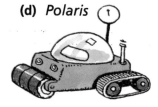

114 metres in
15 seconds

(e) *Mercury*

162 metres in
30 seconds

(f) *Scorpio*

102 metres in
12 seconds

2 List the vehicles in question 1, in order, from fastest to slowest.

3 (a) Find the speed, in metres per second, of each vehicle below.
Write each answer **to the nearest whole number**.

Electra:	110 m in 8 seconds	*Jupiter:*	234 m in 16 seconds
Canaveral:	274 m in 22 seconds	*Canopus:*	125 m in 12 seconds
Gemini:	315 m in 24 seconds	*Ariel:*	211 m in 18 seconds

(b) Alpha Class vehicles can travel at more than 12 metres per second.
Which of these are Alpha Class vehicles?

Work with a partner.

4 (a) Find out how many metres each of you walks in 10 seconds.
(b) Calculate your walking speed in metres per second.

5 Find your running speed in metres per second.

Speed: kilometres per hour

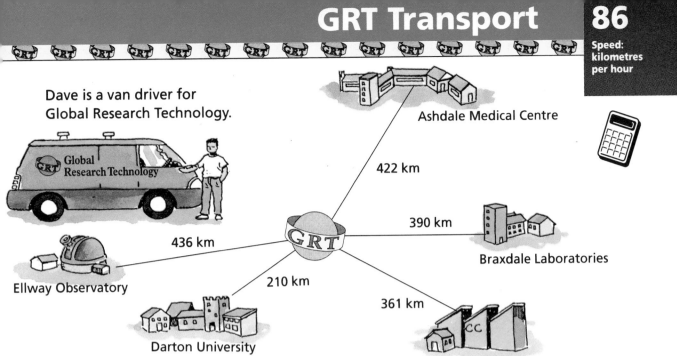

Dave is a van driver for Global Research Technology.

Ashdale Medical Centre

422 km

390 km

Braxdale Laboratories

436 km

GRT

210 km

Ellway Observatory

361 km

Darton University

Conlon Chemicals

Dave took 5 hours to travel from GRT to Ashdale Medical Centre.

In 5 hours he travelled 422 kilometres.

In **1 hour** he travelled 422 ÷ 5 = 84·4 kilometres.

His speed was **84·4 kilometres per hour**.

1 Calculate Dave's speed, in kilometres per hour, for journeys from GRT to

(a) Braxdale Laboratories in 5 hours   (b) Conlon Chemicals in 4 hours

(b) Ellway Observatory in 8 hours   (d) Darton University in 3 hours.

2 Find each speed, in kilometres per hour, **to the nearest whole number**.

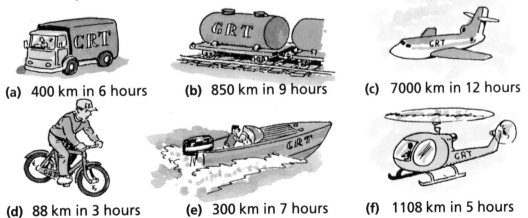

(a) 400 km in 6 hours   (b) 850 km in 9 hours   (c) 7000 km in 12 hours

(d) 88 km in 3 hours   (e) 300 km in 7 hours   (f) 1108 km in 5 hours

3 Clare travels at 35 kilometres per hour. At this speed,

(a) how far will she travel in   • 1 hour   • 2 hours   • 5 hours?

(b) how long would she take to travel from GRT to Darton University?

Problem solving

Ask your teacher what to do next.

R27 H50

Suzy works at Eurotravel.
She leaves home for work at **7.40 am** or **20 to 8 in the morning**.

1 Write these times in two ways.

(a) Suzy arrives at work   **(b)** Eurotravel opens   **(c)** Lunch break   **(d)** Eurotravel closes

(a) clock showing 7:35   (b) `8:45`   (c) clock showing 1:00   (d) `5:15`

Suzy makes up a timetable for the City Tour.

	departs	arrives
Eurotravel to the Castle	8.35 am	8.50 am
Castle to TV Tower	10.45 am	11.00 am
TV Tower to Science Park	12.30 pm	1.15 pm
Science Park to Market	2.40 pm	3.05 pm
Market to Eurotravel	5.35 pm	6.15 pm

2 How many minutes does Suzy allow for travel from

   (a) Eurotravel to the Castle   **(b)** the TV Tower to the Science Park

   (c) the Science Park to the Market   **(d)** the Market to Eurotravel ?

3 How long is spent

   (a) at the Castle   **(b)** in the Science Park   **(c)** at the Market ?

4 How long does the complete City Tour last?

5 Shamina works with Suzy. Find the **finishing time** for each of their tasks.

Suzy	sorting cheques	telephoning	organising tours	booking flights
starts at	9.45 am	10.30 am	11.50 am	3.35 pm
time taken	30 min	1 h 15 min	3 h 20 min	1 h 30 min

Shamina				
starts at	9.35 am	10.20 am	11.55 am	3.10 pm
time taken	40 min	1 h 20 min	2 h 55 min	1 h 40 min

6 Find the **starting time** for each of these tours.

Tour	starts at	lasts for	finishes at
Museum		3 h	12.50 pm
Seaside		4 h 50 min	3.00 pm
Theme Park		3 h 45 min	4.25 pm
Mystery		1 h 10 min	11.05 pm

Eurotravel closes at 5.15 pm

The digital clock shows **24-hour** times.

5.15 pm is written as **17.15**

24-hour times are always written with four figures.

1 Write each of these coach departure times as a 24-hour time.

(a)	Fairground	11 pm	**(b)**	Castle	2 pm
(c)	City Centre	7.25 am	**(d)**	Museum	9.09 am
(e)	Zoo	1.30 pm	**(f)**	Theatre	8.20 pm
(g)	Beach	10.34 am	**(h)**	Art Gallery	2.45 pm

2 Write each time as a 12-hour time. Use am or pm.

(a) 06.10 **(b)** 23.17 **(c)** 12.00 **(d)** 00.50

(e) 08.00 **(f)** 17.00 **(g)** 01.10 **(h)** 16.16

(i) 10.20 **(j)** 18.08

3 Find the missing times.

Coach drivers' finishing times

	12-hour time	24-hour time		12-hour time	24-hour time
Ronnie	8.15 pm	**(a)**	**Maxine**	**(d)**	19.21
Ahmed	**(b)**	10.27	**Varna**	10.06 am	**(e)**
Winston	11.11 pm	**(c)**	**Lee**	**(f)**	13.05

This is a driver's logbook for a day trip to Calais.

time	activity
7.44 am	collected passengers
9.41 am	arrived at port
10.10 am	boarded ferry
11.25 am	arrived in France
12.22 pm	had lunch
1.40 pm	started shopping
4.07 pm	returned to coach
5.18 pm	arrived at port
5.30 pm	boarded ferry
6.49 pm	arrived in UK
8.43 pm	arrived home

4 What happened at

(a) 10.10 **(b)** 13.40 **(c)** 17.18 ?

5 Where were the passengers at

(a) 11.35 **(b)** 17.00 **(c)** 17.45 ?

6 What happened **just before**

(a) 07.45 **(b)** 17.20 **(c)** 20.45 ?

7 What happened **just after**

(a) 09.40 **(b)** 12.20 **(c)** 16.05 ?

H52

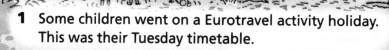
1 Some children went on a Eurotravel activity holiday.
This was their Tuesday timetable.

	swimming	canoeing	lunch	wind-surfing
start	08.30	10.00	12.15	13.45
finish	09.30	12.00	13.15	15.45

(a) How long was spent on each activity?

(b) How long was it from the beginning of swimming to the end of canoeing?

(c) How long was the timetabled day?

2 On Wednesday there was a relay race.
Mark began the race at 10.15. He passed the baton to Sara at 10.31.
Sara passed the baton to David at 10.49.
David crossed the finish line at 11.03.

(a) For how many minutes did each child run?

(b) Who ran for the longest time?

(c) How long did the **team** take to run the relay race?

Tennis Practice – Thursday morning

Ross		Judy		Michael		Moira	
time	activity	time	activity	time	activity	time	activity
09.15	with coach	09.10	serving practice	08.55	watch video	08.55	watch video
10.00	serving practice	09.35	play game	09.35	play game	09.35	serving practice
10.20	ball machine	11.05	with coach	11.05	serving practice	10.00	with coach
10.45	play game	11.50	ball machine	11.35	ball machine	10.45	play game
11.30	watch video	12.10	watch video	11.50	with coach	11.30	ball machine
12.10	lunch	12.50	lunch	12.35	lunch	12.00	lunch

3 (a) How long did Michael spend with the coach?

(b) Who spent most time at
  ● the ball machine   ● serving practice?

(c) Which children do you think played games of tennis
together and for how long?

(d) Which children do you think watched the video
together and for how long?

(e) Make out the Thursday morning timetable
for the tennis coach.

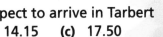

How long should it take me to drive from Glasgow to Tarbert?

It takes about 3 hours.

1 Write, **in 24-hour time**, when Bill could expect to arrive in Tarbert if he leaves Glasgow at   **(a)** 09.30   **(b)** 14.15   **(c)** 17.50

2 Write the arrival time for each person's journey.

	John	Fiona	Steve	May	Jo
leaves at	08.05	07.16	12.00	13.25	17.45
journey time	3 hours	5 hours	2 hours	4 hours	6 hours

How long does it take to travel from Heathrow to London?

The train takes about 50 minutes.

3 Write Jane's expected arrival time in London if she leaves Heathrow at   **(a)** 08.10   **(b)** 14.45   **(c)** 16.25

4 Write each arrival time.

	Ann	Marie	Don	Kate	Hal
leaves at	16.25	07.35	08.20	11.10	18.40
journey time	45 min	50 min	40 min	55 min	35 min

How much time will it take to drive from Calais to Paris?

You need to allow about $5\frac{1}{4}$ hours.

5 Write Jim's expected arrival time in Paris if he leaves Calais at
(a) 07.25   **(b)** 11.05   **(c)** 13.15   **(d)** 16.45

6 **Do Workbook page 16, question 1.**

7 Write each arrival time.

	Donna	Dave	Norman	Sharon	Cara
leaves at	06.20	11.20	12.35	14.50	17.45
journey time	4 h 50 min	3 h 45 min	5 h 30 min	3 h 25 min	5 h 40 min

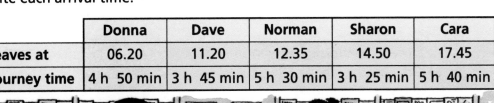

1 **(a)** Write the check-in time for each of these flights.

Eurotravel Information

Domestic flights

Check-in time

1 hour before departure

Boarding time

20 minutes before departure.

Have a good journey.

DOMESTIC FLIGHTS

Flight	Destination	Departure time
AK 421	Manchester	1145
FO 313	London Heathrow	1230
EB 543	Belfast	1255
AX 417	Edinburgh	1320
AK 321	East Midlands	1405
FO 444	Islay	1510
AE 221	London Gatwick	1515

(b) Write the boarding time for each flight.

2 **Do Workbook page 16, question 2.**

3 Write the check-in time for each of these flights.

Eurotravel Information

International flights

Check-in time

1 hour 45 minutes before departure.

Travel with us again.

INTERNATIONAL FLIGHTS

Flight	Destination	Departure time
FK 117	Oslo	1955
AB 183	Geneva	2050
CD 362	Amsterdam	2100
UM 519	Copenhagen	2215
AB 118	Paris	2225
FK 326	Madrid	2305
XT 478	Stockholm	2320

4 An Edinburgh to Birmingham flight
  • usually takes 1 hour 15 minutes
  • took 20 minutes longer today
  • arrived at 13.10
When did the plane leave Edinburgh?

5 A Glasgow to London flight
  • was delayed by 1 hour 15 minutes
  • took 1 hour 20 minutes
  • arrived at 15.05
At what time **should** the plane have left Glasgow?

R29 H55

Ask your teacher what to do next.

A right angle is 90°

A straight angle is 180°

An acute angle is less than 90°

An obtuse angle is between 90° and 180°

A reflex angle is between 180° and 360°

1 Do Workbook pages 29 and 30.

2 Measure each of the angles marked on this walk through Avonside Park.

3 (a) Draw a line 10 cm long.

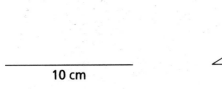

10 cm

(b) Draw angles as shown.

30° 75°
10 cm

(c) Complete the triangle.

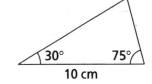

30° 75°
10 cm

(d) Measure the size of the third angle.

4 (a) Draw a triangle which has these sizes.

(b) Measure the size of the third angle.

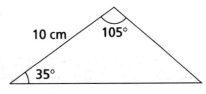

10 cm 105°

35°

R30 H56

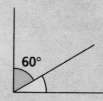

Dan is the gardener at Avonside Park.
He calculates angle sizes to help him
lay out the gardens.

60°

The red and blue angles
make one right angle or 90°.
The blue angle is 90° – 60°
= **30°**

1 Each diagram shows a right angle.
Calculate the size of each blue angle.

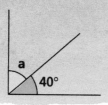
a 40°

55° b

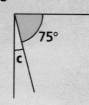
75° c

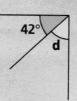
42° d

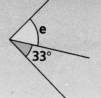
e 33°

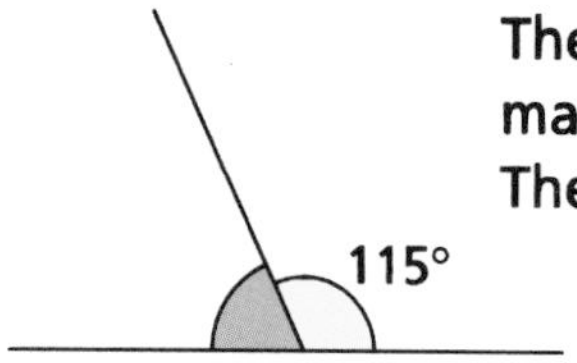

The green and yellow angles
make one straight angle or 180°.
The green angle is 180° – 115°
= **65°**

115°

2 Calculate the size of each green angle.

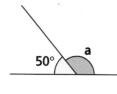
50° a

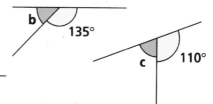
b 135°

c 110°

d 46°

104° e

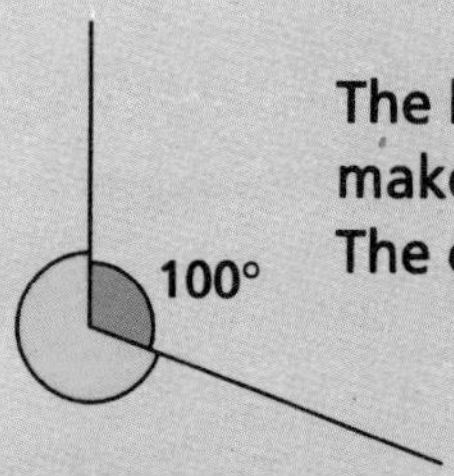

The brown and orange angles
make one full turn or 360°.
The orange angle is 360° – 100°
= **260°**

100°

3 Calculate the size of each orange angle.

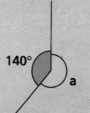
140° a

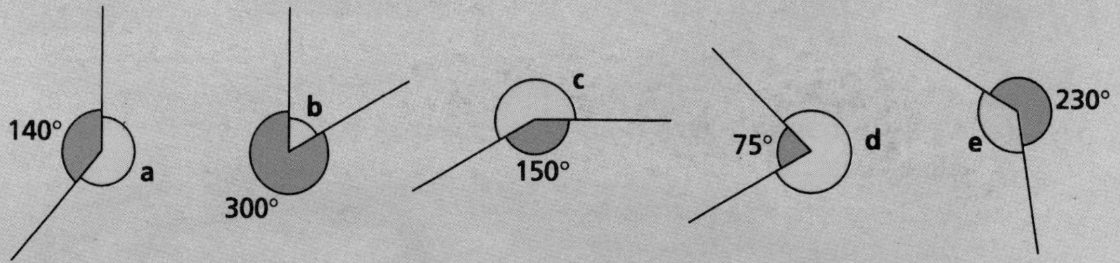

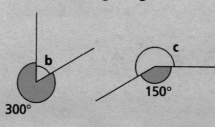
b 300°

c 150°

75° d

e 230°

The red angle shows a turn of
3 right angles or 270° clockwise from North.

1 Describe each of these turns in
right angles and in degrees.

(a) 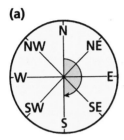 **(b)** 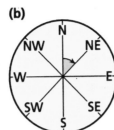 **(c)** 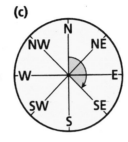 **(d)**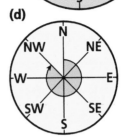

2 (a) Place a pencil pointing North on top of the green compass. Turn it through
90° clockwise. In which direction is the pencil pointing?

(b) Find the finishing direction for these clockwise turns from North:
  • through 4 right angles   • through 225°

Bearings are measured **clockwise from North** and used to give directions.
The number of degrees is always given using **three figures**.

This plane is flying
on the bearing 240°

240°

This boat is sailing
on the bearing 070°

70°

---

3 Copy and complete this table.

Compass direction	N	NE	E	SE	S	SW	W	NW
Bearing	000°	045°						

4 This direction indicator
in Avonside Park is
marked in 10° intervals.
Find the bearing of
each place.
Record like this:

Changing Rooms 100°

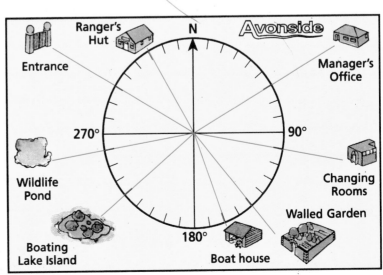

The Boathouse

N

1 **You need a protractor.**
Measure each red angle.
Write the bearing of the
Boathouse from each place.
Record like this:
From Ranger's Hut 150°

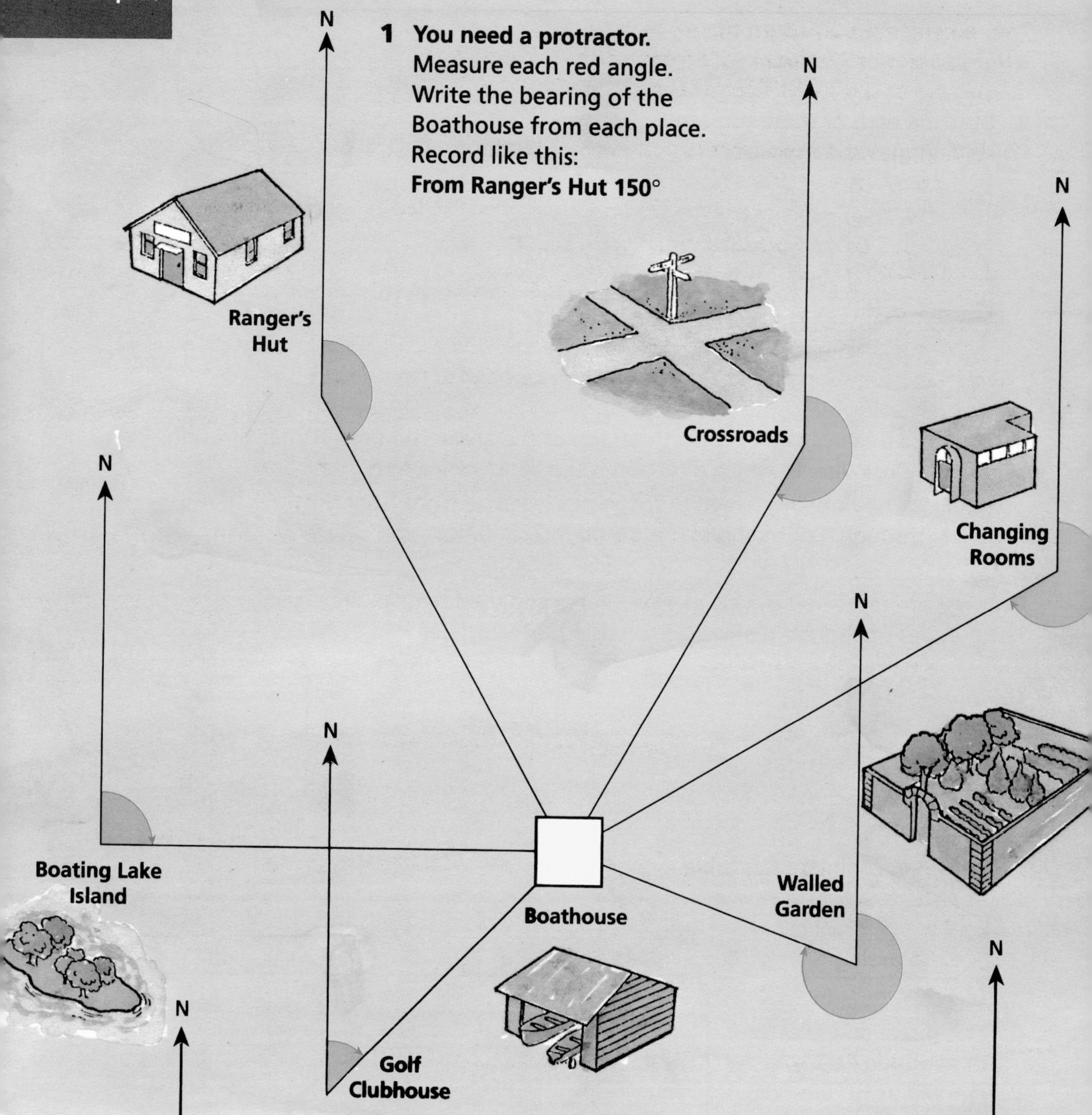

**Ranger's
Hut**

N

N

N

Crossroads

**Changing
Rooms**

N

N

N

**Boating Lake
Island**

Boathouse

**Walled
Garden**

N

N

**Golf
Clubhouse**

2 Find the bearing of
  (a) the Ranger's Hut from the Entrance
  (b) the Entrance from the Ranger's Hut.

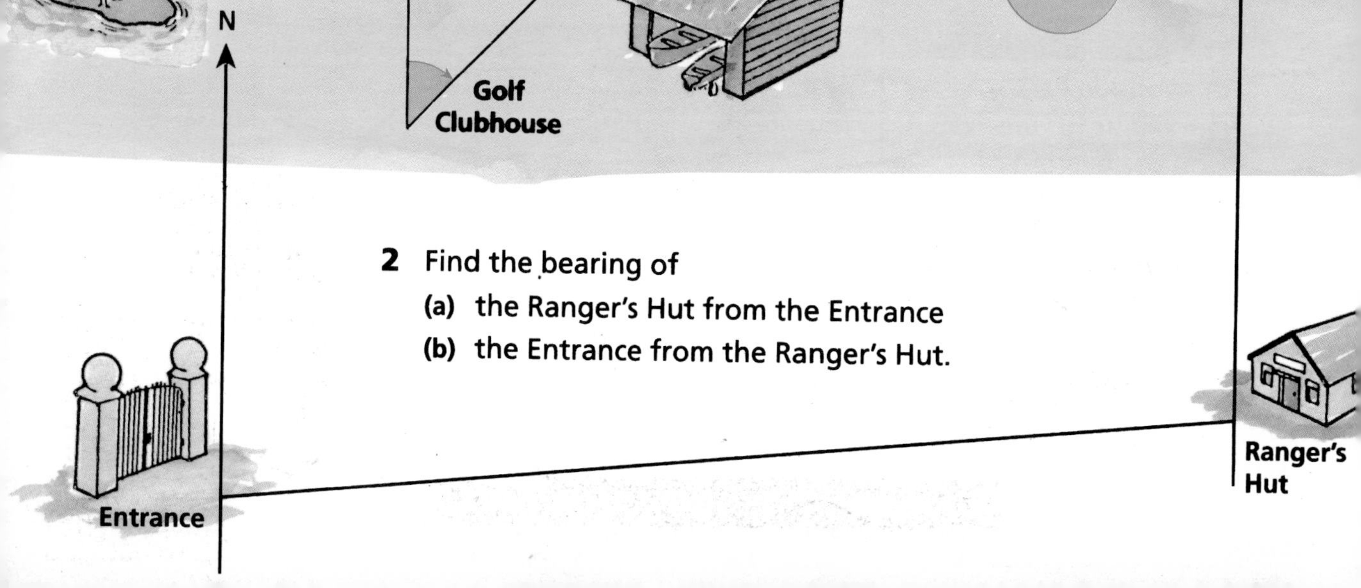

Entrance

**Ranger's
Hut**

You need a ruler and a protractor.
The plan shows the orienteering course at Avonside Park.
It is drawn to a scale of **1 cm to 200 m.**

1 (a) Copy and complete the table to describe the course using **distances** and **bearings**.

	Distance	Bearing
Start to A	1600 m	035°
A to B		

(b) Find the total length of the course in kilometres and metres.

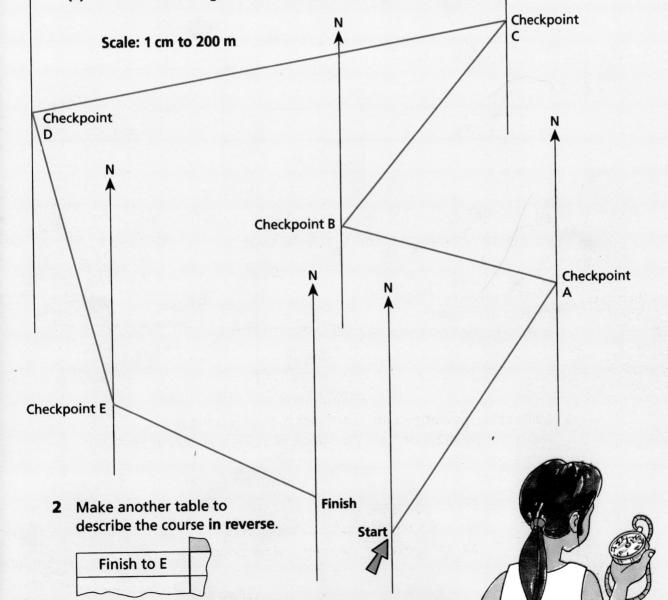

Scale: 1 cm to 200 m

2 Make another table to describe the course **in reverse.**

Finish to E

Designs

Do Workbook page 17.

1 Trace each design and colour it as shown.
How often does the design fit its outline in one full turn? What do you notice?

(a) 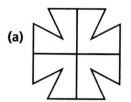 **(b)** 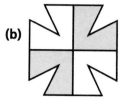 **(c)** 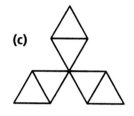 **(d)**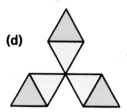

2 (a) • Cut out the blue shape from the
bottom of **Workbook page 20**.

• On plain paper draw two lines like this
at right angles.

• Draw round the blue shape in the
positions shown.

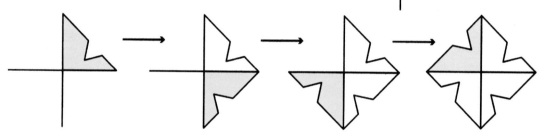

(b) How often does your design fit its outline in one full turn?

(c) Colour your design so that it only fits twice.

3 Make a coloured design with
rotational symmetry.
Start with the blue shape like this:

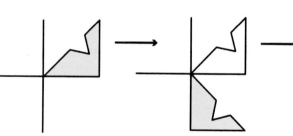

4 Make coloured designs with rotational symmetry using the
red or the green shape from **Workbook page 20** or shapes of your own.

Ask your teacher what to do next.

1 (a) Draw a shape like this on card. Cut it out.

(b) Slide your shape and draw round it to make patterns like these.

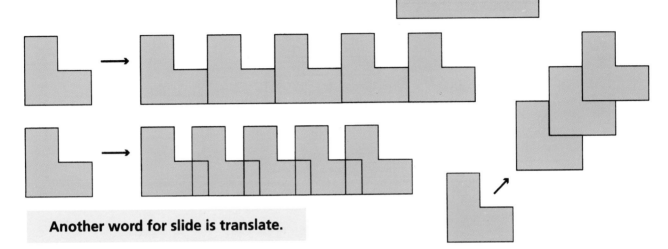

Another word for slide is translate.

2 Make your own shape. Translate it to make patterns.

Work as a group.

3 (a) Each cut out the tiles from **Workbook page 18**.

(b) Fit the tiles together to make these patterns.

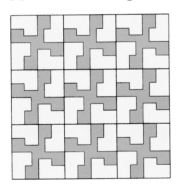 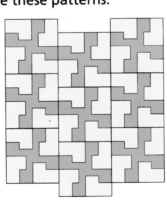 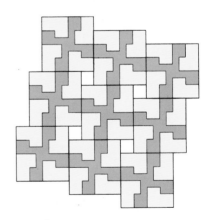

(c) Make different patterns with the tiles.

(d) Stick the tiles on a large sheet of paper to show the pattern you like best.

4 (a) Decide as a group how to colour the square tiles on **Workbook page 20** so that they are all identical.

(b) Colour the tiles and cut them out.

(c) Make a pattern. Stick the tiles on a large sheet of paper.

(d) Do this again for the triangular tiles on **Workbook page 20**.

Ask your teacher what to do next.

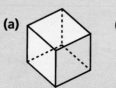 (a)
 (b)
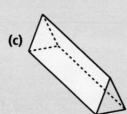 (c)
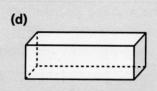 (d)
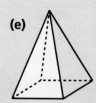 (e)

1 Name each shape and match it to its net below.

Record like this   (a) cube ⟶ net _____ .

Nets

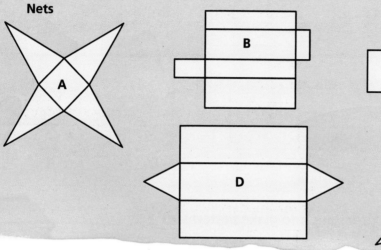

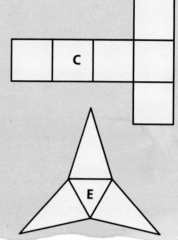

All these shapes are **pyramids**.

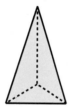
triangular pyramid
(tetrahedron)

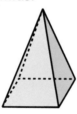
square
pyramid

pentagonal
pyramid

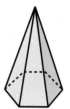
hexagonal
pyramid

2 (a) Work as a group. Use shapes to make these four pyramids.

(b) Copy and complete this table for your pyramids.

Shape	Number of faces	Number of vertices	Number of edges
triangular pyramid	4		

(c) What do you notice about the number of faces and vertices?

(d) Use the patterns in your table.
Copy and complete these rows for the next two pyramids.

heptagonal pyramid	8		
octagonal pyramid			

Work as a group.
All these shapes are **prisms.**

triangular
prism

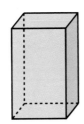
rectangular
prism (cuboid)

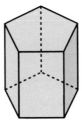
pentagonal
prism

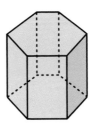
hexagonal
prism

3 **(a)** Use shapes to make these four prisms.

(b) Copy and complete this table for your prisms.

Shape	Number of faces	Number of vertices	Number of edges
triangular prism	5		

(c) Use the patterns in your table.
Copy and complete these rows for the next two prisms.

heptagonal prism			
octagonal prism			

4 Use squares and equilateral triangles.

(a) Make this net.
Fold it to make a 3D shape.
This 3D shape is called an **octahedron**.

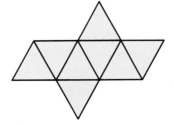

(b) Make two congruent square pyramids.
Use them to make an octahedron
like the one in **(a)**.

Ask your teacher what to do next.

Use the shapes on Workbook page 22.

Here are three ways to find out about shapes.

By folding

1 **(a)** Cut out the rhombus.

   (b) Fold along its lines of symmetry and compare
   the side lengths and the angle sizes.

   (c) Stick the shape in your exercise book.

   (d) Copy and complete:

   A rhombus has _____ equal sides.

   Its opposite angles are _____.

By tracing and turning

2 **(a)** Trace the square.

   (b) Rotate the tracing and compare
   the side lengths and the angle sizes.

   (c) Cut out the square and stick
   it in your exercise book.

   (d) Copy and complete:

   A square has _____ equal sides.

   It has _____ equal angles.

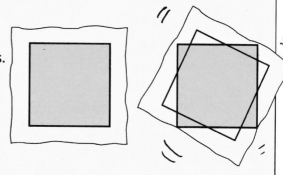

By measuring

You need a ruler and a protractor.

3 **(a)** Measure the sides and angles of the isosceles triangle.

   (b) Cut out the triangle and stick it in your exercise book.

   (c) Copy and complete:

   An isosceles triangle has _____ equal sides.

   It has _____ equal angles.

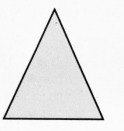

4 Use folding, tracing and turning, or measuring.
Find out and write about the sides and angles of the
   (a) rectangle   **(b)** equilateral triangle
   (c) kite   **(d)** parallelogram.

5 Which three- or four-sided shape is each person thinking about?

(a) It has two pairs of equal sides and only one pair of equal angles.

(b) It has one pair of equal angles and only three sides.

(c) Its opposite sides and its opposite angles are equal. It has no line of symmetry.

(d) It has four equal angles and only two lines of symmetry.

(e) It fits its outline in exactly three ways in a full turn.

6 (a) Which three- or four-sided shapes **could** each of these clues describe?

red shape
Clue
It has two pairs of equal angles.

blue shape
Clue
All of its sides are equal.

green shape
Clue
It has only one pair of equal angles.

Problem solving

(b) Write a second clue for each so that there is **only one** possible
   • red shape • blue shape • green shape.

R31 H59

1 A **diagonal** is a straight line joining two corners of a shape that are not next to each other.
Which of these red lines are diagonals?

   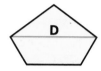 

2 (a) Sketch a square and show its **2** diagonals.

(b) Sketch and name 3 different shapes, each with **only 2** diagonals.

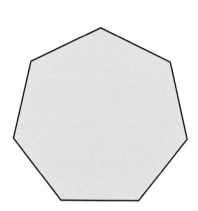

3 (a) Sketch this 7-sided shape.

(b) Choose **one** corner. Find, by drawing, how many diagonals there are from this corner.

(c) How many diagonals altogether do you **think** the shape has? Check by drawing.

Problem solving **4** Draw a shape with **exactly 9** diagonals.

You need strips and fasteners.

5 (a) Make each of these frameworks.

(b) A framework which cannot easily be pushed out of shape is **rigid**.
Which of your frameworks is rigid?

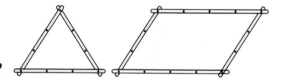

6 Extra strips can be used to make a framework rigid.

(a) Which of these ways do you **think** will make the parallelogram rigid?

(b) Check using strips and sketch any framework which is rigid.

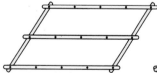 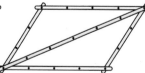 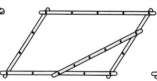 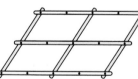

(c) Do all of this again for these pentagons.

 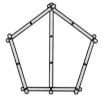  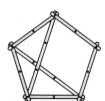

7 A **triangular** framework is rigid.
Colour the triangles in your sketches.

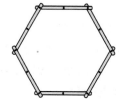

Problem solving **8** Find, then sketch, two different ways to make a hexagon rigid using **exactly 3** diagonals.

You need 2 long strips
and 2 short strips.

1 Use 1 long and 1 short strip as diagonals of a shape.
- Join the strips as shown.
- Mark the ends of each diagonal.
- What shape do you **think** is made when the ends are joined by straight lines?
- Check by completing the drawing of the shape.

2 Repeat question **1** starting with the strips like this:

(a)

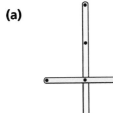

(b)

3 Use 2 equal strips as diagonals of a shape.
Repeat question **1** starting with the strips like this:

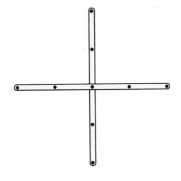

4 (a) **Use centimetre squared paper**. Draw diagonals like these:

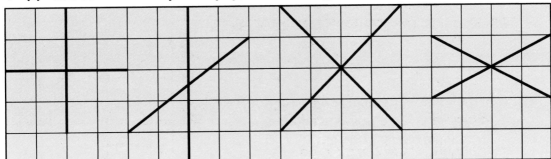

(b) Join the ends of the diagonals and name each shape you make.

(c) What do you notice about the lengths of the diagonals of squares and rectangles?

What's my line?

Lines which are always the same distance apart are **parallel**.

These lines are parallel.

These lines are **not** parallel.

1 **(a)** Draw a line on each side of your ruler.

(b) Are these lines parallel?

2 Which streets are parallel to

(a) Bread Street

(b) Main Street

(c) Strathaven Road?

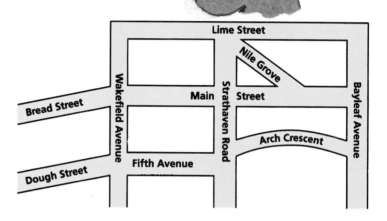

You need centimetre squared paper.

3 **(a)** Draw and label a grid like this.

(b) Mark these points on the grid and join them, in order, with straight lines. (0,1) (1,3) (4,3) (3,1) and back to (0,1)

(c) What shape have you drawn?

(d) How many **pairs** of parallel lines does it have?

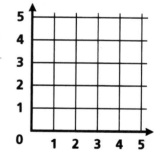

4 Repeat question 3 for these points:

(a) (0,1) (1,4) (4,4) (5,1) and back to (0,1)

(b) (0,3) (2,4) (4,3) (2,0) and back to (0,3)

Problem solving

5 **(a)** Draw three grids and mark 5 red points on each as shown.

(b) Mark one more point on each grid so that, when all 6 points are joined, you have a **hexagon** with
• 3 pairs • 2 pairs • 1 pair of parallel sides.

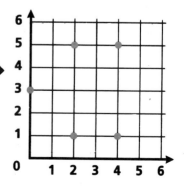

Ask your teacher what to do next.

You need a pair of compasses.

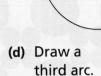

4 cm

1 (a) Draw a circle with radius 4 cm.

(b) With the same radius, draw an arc.

(c) Draw a second arc.

(d) Draw a third arc.

(e) Continue to complete the flower design.

centre

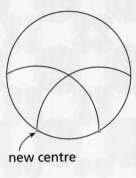

new centre

new centre

(f) Colour your design.

2 (a) Draw another circle with radius 4 cm.

(b) With the same radius, make a mark on the circumference.

(c) Continue making marks round the circumference.

(d) Put a dot at each mark.

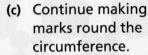

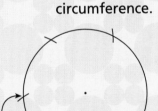

centre

new centre

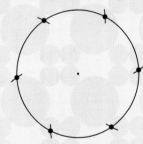

(e) With straight lines, join each dot to every other dot. Colour your design.

3 Use centimetre squared paper. Copy this design and colour it.

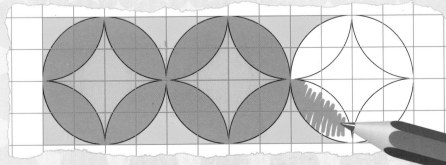

4 Draw and colour your own circle designs.

What's the question?

Write **two questions** about each shape
• one whose answer is **A**
• one whose answer is **B**.

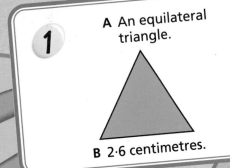

1
A An equilateral triangle.
B 2·6 centimetres.

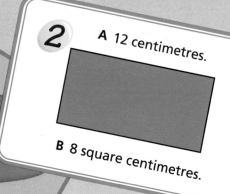

2
A 12 centimetres.
B 8 square centimetres.

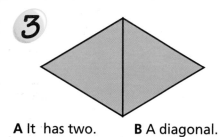

3
A It has two.   **B** A diagonal.

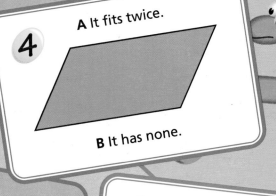

4
A It fits twice.
B It has none.

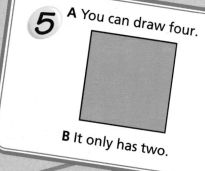

5
A You can draw four.
B It only has two.

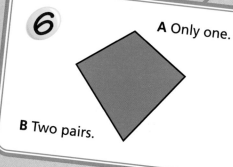

6
A Only one.
B Two pairs.

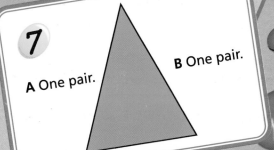

7
A One pair.
B One pair.

Ask your teacher what to do next.

The schools in Beckford are taking part in a Bike Awareness Week.
Thirty children from Fortview School complete questionnaires about their bikes.

This is a **summary** of all the data.

BAW QUESTIONNAIRE Name: Fortview School

Type of bike	Mountain 14	Racer 6	BMX 8	other 2
Number of gears	less than 6 5	10 – 12 8	more than 12 17	
Style of handlebars	14	6	6	other 4
Colour of bike	white 10	silver 8	red 6	blue 2	other 4
Accessories	mudguards 8	lights 26	pump 12	water bottle 18

1 **(a)** What is the most common
   • type of bike   • style of handlebars?

   (b) What is the least common
   • accessory   • colour of bike?

   (c) How many bikes have more than 5 gears?

   (d) What fraction of the bikes have
   • dropped handlebars (↪)   • water bottles?

   (e) Why are more than 30 responses recorded for accessories?

Work as a group.
Ask your teacher for 21 copies of the BAW QUESTIONNAIRE

2 Ask 20 people who have a bike each to complete a questionnaire.

3 Make a summary of the data on the blank questionnaire.

4 For **your** data   **(a)** repeat question **1**   **(b)** write four facts.

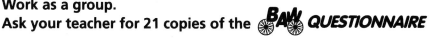

What age were you when you had your first bike?

These graphs show the answers given by
• girls • boys • girls **and** boys.

1 (a) How many girls answered?
  (b) How many girls did not give an age as an answer?
  (c) Which answer is the mode?

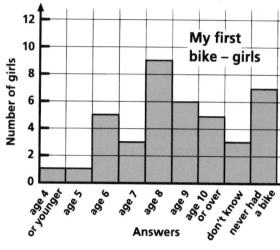

2 (a) How many boys answered?
  (b) How many boys were 8 or older when they had their first bike?
  (c) Which answer is the mode?

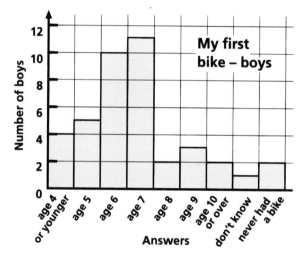

3 (a) How many children
    • did not give an age
    • gave an age?
  (b) Which answer is the mode?

Problem solving 4 Use centimetre squared paper. Redraw this graph so that it shows **clearly**
  • answers given by girls
  • answers given by boys.

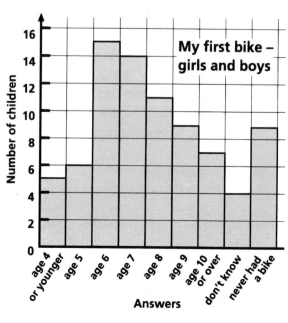

Go to Workbook page 31.

Do you always put your hands on the handlebar grips?

Do you always pedal with the balls of your feet?

Do you always sit on the saddle?

The graph shows Class 7's answers.

1 (a) How many children answered each question?

(b) Which good habit did
- most of Class 7 have
- fewest of Class 7 have?

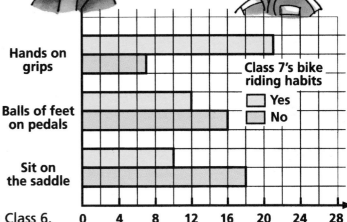

Here are some bike safety answers from Class 6.

I always wear a helmet.

I sometimes signal to other road users.

I never check my brakes.

I sometimes wear something fluorescent.

The graph shows all of Class 6's responses.

2 (a) How many children answered each question?

(b) What fraction of the children
- always give signals
- sometimes wear a helmet
- never check their brakes?

(c) What advice would you give to these children to improve their bike safety habits?

3 Draw a graph using this data from Class 5.

Do you	always	sometimes	never
cycle to school?	1	3	27
cycle near home?	24	4	3
cycle on holiday?	5	14	12

On your bike

This pie chart shows the types of bike owned by children in Denvale School.

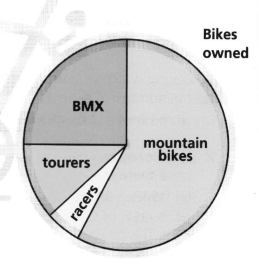

Bikes owned

1 Which type of bike is owned by
   • most children   • fewest children?

2 Write true or false for each statement.
   (a) More than half the bikes owned are mountain bikes.
   (b) More children own tourers than BMX bikes.
   (c) Less than a quarter of the bikes owned are racers.

Ten children were asked which of these bikes they preferred.

Stomper   **Powertrak**   **Hopper**   **Trekker**

The pie chart shows their preferred bike.

Preferred bike

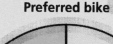
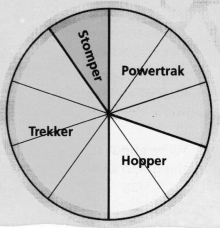

3 Into how many **equal** parts has the circle been divided?

4 How many pupils preferred the
   (a) Stomper   (b) Powertrak
   (c) Hopper   (d) Trekker?

5 What **fraction** of the pupils preferred the
   (a) Stomper   (b) Powertrak
   (c) Hopper   (d) Trekker?

Favourite bike colours

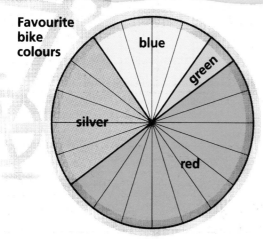

6 This pie chart shows the favourite bike colours of 20 children. How many chose
   (a) red   (b) green
   (c) silver   (d) blue?

7 What fraction of the children chose
   (a) red   (b) green
   (c) silver   (d) blue?

Go to Workbook page 32.

This trend graph shows the number of accidents involving cyclists over a
ten year period in Beckford.

1 During which year was
the number of accidents
(a) highest   **(b)** lowest?

2 How many accidents
were there in
(a) 1987   **(b)** 1992
(c) 1995?

3 In which year was the
number of accidents
(a) 17   **(b)** 7
(c) 12?

4 In which year do you
think the first cycle way
was opened in Beckford?

5 Write about the trend
the graph shows.

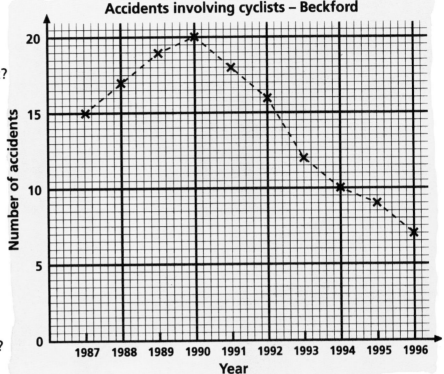

Accidents involving cyclists – Beckford

This trend graph shows the
number of accidents involving
cyclists in Caldwell.

6 Write about the trend
the graph shows.

7 You need 2 mm
graph paper.

(a) Use the data in the
table to draw a
trend graph for
cycle accidents in
Dunforth.

(b) Write about the trend
your graph shows.

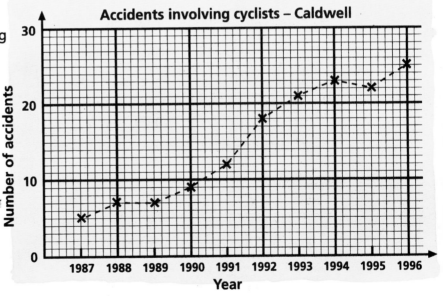

Accidents involving cyclists – Caldwell

Accidents involving cyclists – Dunforth									
Year	'87	'88	'89	'90	'91	'92	'93	'94	'95	'96
Number of accidents	9	10	9	11	20	13	11	8	5	3

During Beckford's Bike Awareness Week some special events take place.

1 Here are the scores of 7 cyclists in **Round 1** of the Wheelie competition.

12 12 14 16 17 17 17

(a) What is the difference between the lowest and highest scores?

This difference is called the **range**.

(b) Which score is midway between the lowest and highest scores?

When the scores are **ordered** the middle one is called the **median**.

(c) Which score occurs most often?

The score which occurs most frequently is called the **mode**.

(d) What is the **mean** score?

The total of the scores divided by the number of scores is called the **mean**.

2 (a) For the scores in each of these rounds, find
  • the range   • the median   • the mode   • the mean.

	Alice	Bobby	Corrie	Dave	Elda	Farah	Graham
Round 2	21	21	21	22	23	26	27
Round 3	17	25	18	23	23	15	19
Round 4	23	20	28	32	29	23	27

(b) In which round was the range of scores greatest?

(c) In Round 2, how many cyclists had a score
  • lower than the median   • higher than the median?

(d) In Round 3, how many cyclists had a score
  • lower than the mode   • higher than the mode?

(e) In Round 4, how many cyclists had a score
  • lower than the mean   • higher than the mean?

(f) Who had the median score in Round 3 **and** in Round 4?

(g) Who had the mean score in Round 2?

(h) Who had the mean score in Round 3? Explain.

Go to Workbook page 33.

Children from Fortview school took part in a cycle-cross.
Points are awarded to those who complete each stage.

Stage 1 points					
3	12	6	9	12	15
22	18	5	14	20	12
13	7	13	16	20	10
19	21	18	5	15	23
20	8	10	7	9	3
11	4	15	16	13	19

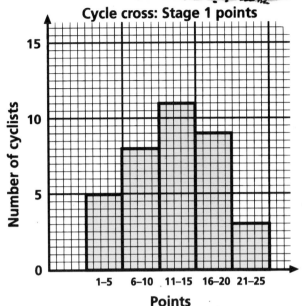

Cycle cross: Stage 1 points

1 **(a)** How many cyclists scored
points in Stage 1?

(b) What is the range of points?

In the graph, points are
grouped in **class intervals**.

2 **(a)** How many class intervals are shown on the graph?

(b) How many cyclists are there in the class interval • 1–5 • 16–20?

(c) How many cyclists scored • less than 11 points • more than 15 points?

3 **Do Workbook page 34.**

The graph shows each cyclist's time,
to the nearest minute, for Stage 4.

4 How many cyclists took part?

5 Use the class intervals from
the Stage 4 graph.

(a) Make a frequency table
for these Stage 5 times.

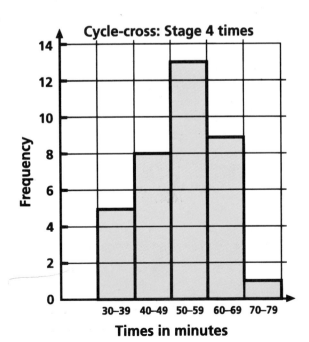

Cycle-cross: Stage 4 times

Stage 5 times					
63	38	40	43	55	60
71	52	33	45	52	56
62	58	57	54	72	45
50	44	52	58	65	41
53	57	55	64	40	39

(b) Draw a graph.

(c) How many cyclists' times were • 50 minutes or longer
• 49 minutes or shorter?

R32 H64

Work as a group.

1

How safety conscious are cyclists in your school?

(a) List about six more questions like these so that you find out how safety conscious they are.

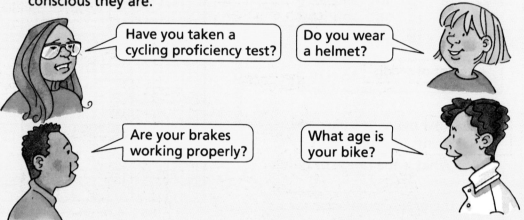

Have you taken a cycling proficiency test?

Do you wear a helmet?

Are your brakes working properly?

What age is your bike?

(b) Think about the answers the cyclists might give.
Decide how these could be recorded.

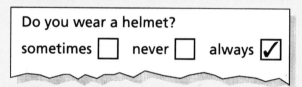

Do you wear a helmet?

sometimes ☐ never ☐ always ✓

How old is your bike?
less than 1 year old _____
1–2 years old
more than
2 years old _____ ✓

Name	Yes	No	Don't know
		✓	

(c) Design a questionnaire.

(d) Ask **20** cyclists each to fill in a copy of your questionnaire.

(e) Use the data you have gathered to make a display.

Safe Clothes

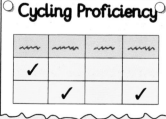

Cycling Proficiency

Our Cyclists

(f) List **five** facts you have found from your survey.

(g) Suggest two ways in which cyclists in your school could become more safety conscious.

Work as a group.

BAW 2

Facts about your bike.

(a) Find the following information about **5 bikes**.

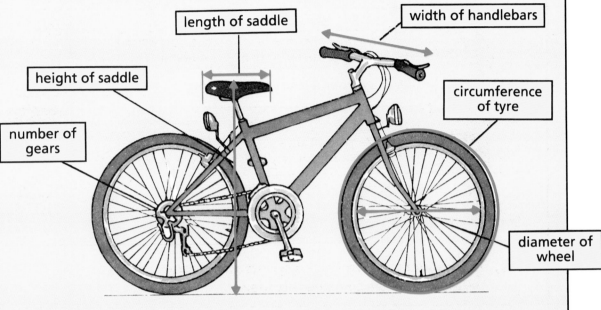

length of saddle

width of handlebars

height of saddle

circumference of tyre

number of gears

diameter of wheel

(b) Copy and complete the table.

Name	Type of bike	Number of gears	Height of saddle				

(c) Choose three sets of data. Calculate the mean for each.

BAW 3

Cycle park

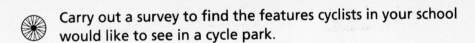 Carry out a survey to find the features cyclists in your school would like to see in a cycle park.

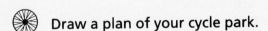 Draw a plan of your cycle park.

 Make a poster to tell others about your cycle park.

Ask your teacher what to do next.

Tile maker

You need card rectangles, scissors and sticky tape.

1 (a) Draw a triangle like this at one end of a card rectangle.

(b) Cut out the triangle. Stick it at the opposite end of the rectangle to make a tile.

(c) Use your tile. Draw round it to make a tiling.

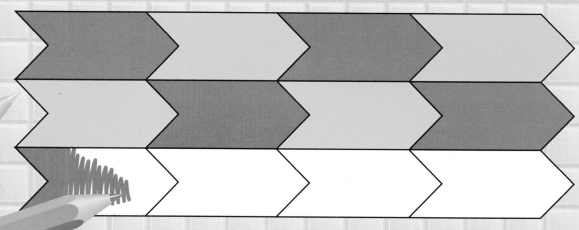

(d) Colour your tiling.

2 Make your own tiles and draw tilings with them.

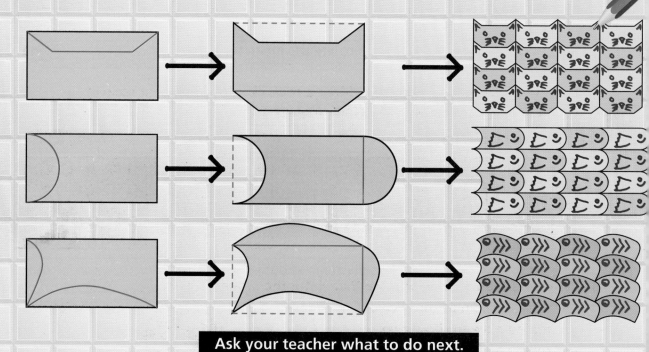

Ask your teacher what to do next.

1 Debbie, Elaine and Jason talked about what might happen at the fair.
Describe how likely they thought each of these events would be.

| Debbie ringing the bell on the strength machine | Jason hitting 2 coconuts | Elaine eating candy floss | Debbie hitting 1 coconut | Jason screaming on the Rollercoaster |

impossible — very unlikely — unlikely — likely — very likely — certain

There are 20 squares on this grid.
10 of them give a win.
The other 10 lose.

The chance or **probability** of a WIN is
10 in 20 or **1 in 2** or $\frac{1}{2}$

This can be shown on
a probability scale like this:

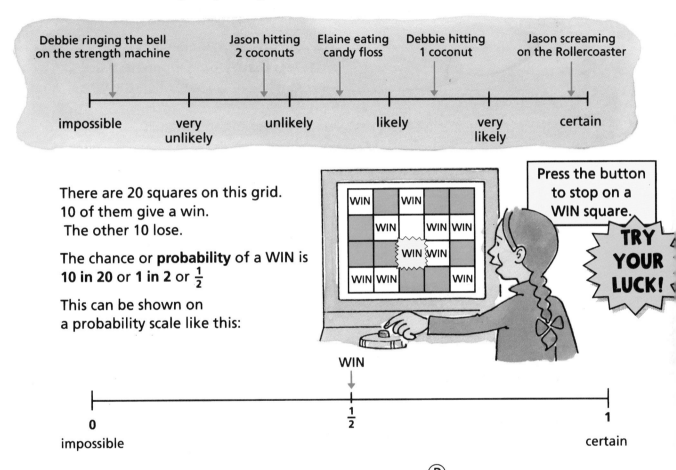

Press the button to stop on a WIN square.

TRY YOUR LUCK!

WIN

0 — $\frac{1}{2}$ — 1
impossible — certain

2 Draw your own probability scale. Mark arrows like this ⓟ on your scale to
estimate the probability of a WIN on these grids.

WIN on blue   WIN on red   WIN on green ✱   WIN on ●

P   Q   R   S

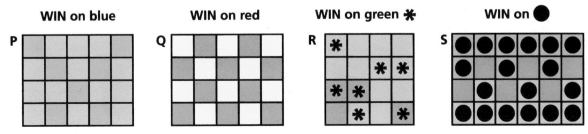

3 Write **less than** $\frac{1}{2}$ or $\frac{1}{2}$ or **more than** $\frac{1}{2}$ for the probability of
   (a) tossing a coin to show **tails**
   (b) rolling a die to show a **six**
   (c) rolling a die to show a **number less than 5**.

WHEEL OF
FORTUNE

1 List **all** the possible numbers the pointer
could show if the wheel stopped at

(a) a number greater than 20

(b) an odd number

(c) a square number

(d) a multiple of 7

(e) a factor of 36.

2 Use your answers to question 1.
Write **less than** $\frac{1}{2}$ or $\frac{1}{2}$ or **more than** $\frac{1}{2}$
for the probability that, when the wheel stops,
the pointer shows

(a) a number greater than 20

(b) an odd number

(c) a square number

(d) a multiple of 7

(e) a factor of 36.

Throw one dart –
hit any card to win

33 26 31 29

28 30 32 27 34

3 List **all** the possible numbers if the card hit shows

(a) an odd number

(b) an even number

(c) a number between 25 and 35

(d) a square number

(e) a multiple of 5.

4 Use your answers to question 3.
Write **0** or **less than** $\frac{1}{2}$ or $\frac{1}{2}$ or **more than** $\frac{1}{2}$ or **1**
for the probability that the card hit shows

(a) an odd number (b) an even number

(c) a number between 25 and 35 (d) a square number

(e) a multiple of 5.

☠ Flatten a Pirate

5 Write **0** or **less than** $\frac{1}{2}$ or $\frac{1}{2}$ or **more than** $\frac{1}{2}$ or **1**
for the probability that a pirate knocked over will have

(a) a striped shirt (b) a hat (c) a beard

(d) an eye-patch (e) a blue hat (f) an eye-patch and a red beard.

★ Lucky Draw ★

There are 8 coloured balls in each machine.

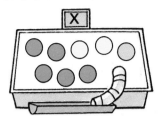 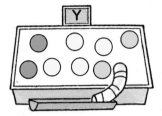 

1 For each machine, X, Y and Z

    (a) write **0** or **less than** $\frac{1}{2}$ or $\frac{1}{2}$ or **more than** $\frac{1}{2}$ or **1** for the probability of drawing a **red** ball.

    (b) explain how you could make the probability of drawing a red ball $\frac{1}{2}$.

2 Explain how you could make the probability of drawing a **green** ball from machine X **more than** $\frac{1}{2}$.

3 **(a)** Use triangular paper, card and a cocktail stick to make a spinner like this. ⟶

    (b) Spin it 30 times and record your results. Is your spinner fair? Explain.

    (c) Put some Blutack on the **back of number 2**. Spin again 30 times and record your results. Is the spinner fair? Explain.

    (d) Explain how to put Blutack onto your spinner so that the probability of landing on an odd number is **more than** $\frac{1}{2}$. Spin to check.

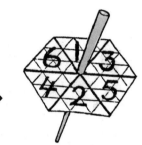

4 There is **no Blutack** on **any** of these spinners.

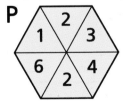 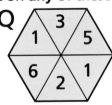 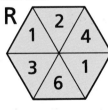 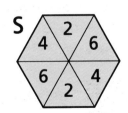

> **Odds –**
> you
> win!
>
> **Evens –**
> you
> lose!

    (a) Describe the probability that each spinner will land on an odd number.

    (b) Which spinner gives an equal chance of landing on an odd or even number?

    (c) Explain how you could change the other spinners so that each gives an equal chance of landing on an odd or even number.

Ask your teacher what to do next.

H65

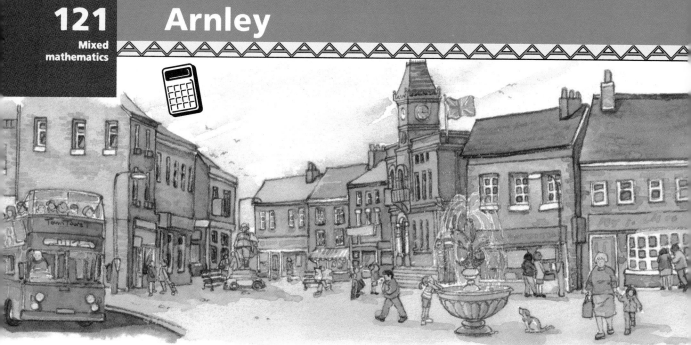

1 The population of Arnley is 37 254. On 2nd May, 8400 tourists visited the town. 40% of the tourists were foreign.

 (a) Find the total population, including tourists, on 2nd May.
   Round this total to the nearest thousand.

 (b) What percentage of the tourists were **not** foreign?

 (c) Calculate the number of foreign tourists.

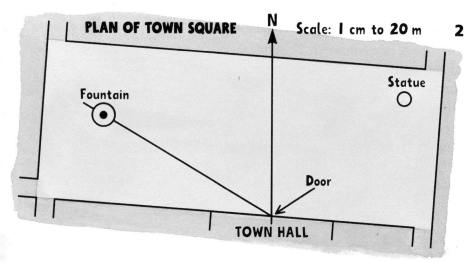

PLAN OF TOWN SQUARE N Scale: 1 cm to 20 m

Statue

Fountain

Door

TOWN HALL

2 (a) Measure the bearing of the fountain from the door of the Town Hall.

 (b) The statue weighs 750 kg less than 2 tonnes. What is its weight?

 (c) Find the perimeter of the town square in **metres**.

3 (a) Copy and complete this timetable for all the Town Tours in one day. **Use 24-hour times.**

Tour starts	Tour finishes

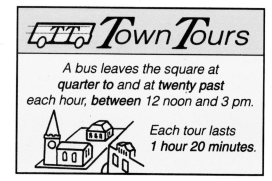

Town Tours

A bus leaves the square at quarter to and at twenty past each hour, between 12 noon and 3 pm.

Each tour lasts 1 hour 20 minutes.

 (b) What is the smallest number of buses needed to run the tours each day? Explain.

1 There is a market in the square every Tuesday.
The table shows the number of stalls each week for six weeks.

Week	1	2	3	4	5	6
Number of stalls	72	58	55	60	67	71

(a) Calculate the average number of stalls per week to the
nearest whole number.

(b) In Week 3, the market was on June 11th. Write the
market dates for the other five weeks.

(c) In week 1, eighteen of the stalls sold clothing.
In week 1, what • fraction • percentage
of all the stalls sold clothing?

(d) Each stall is the same size.
How many stalls, in a row, can
be fitted into a length of 50 m?

(e) Calculate the area of ground, in
square metres, taken up by one stall.

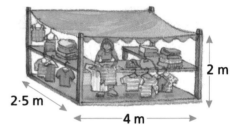

2 (a) Copy this design for Arnley Town
Crest on centimetre squared paper.
Colour it completely.

(b) Describe the symmetry of
• the blue A shape
• the red and yellow star.

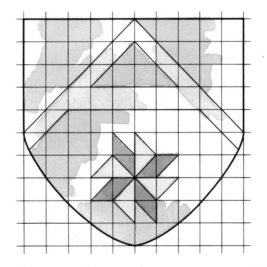

3 A code is used to number the rooms in the Town Hall.

SECOND FLOOR 21 0 ROOM 10

The table shows the number of the **last** room on each of the three floors.

Ground Floor	First Floor	Second Floor
005	106	212

Find how many of each digit 0, 1, 2, ... 9 are needed
for **all** the rooms in the Town Hall.

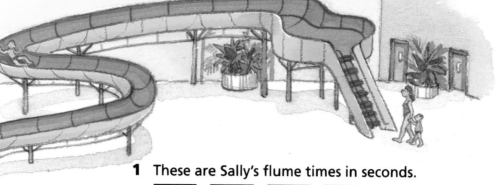

1 These are Sally's flume times in seconds.

| 8·30 | 8·63 | 8·36 | 8·03 | 8·6 |

(a) Put the times in order starting with the fastest.
(b) What is the difference between her fastest and slowest times?
(c) Find her • median time • mean time.

2 The floor of the swimming pool can be raised or lowered to change the depth of the water for swimming. Calculate the volume of water when the depth is
(a) 2 metres (b) 1·8 metres (c) 1·5 metres.

3 Al swam 18 lengths of the pool in 30 minutes.
Calculate (a) his rate in **lengths per minute**
(b) his speed in **metres per minute**.

25 m

16 m

16 m

4 Calculate, in **metres per minute**, to the nearest whole number, the speed of each swimmer.

Times for swimming 1000 m	
Tom	59 minutes
Sally	61 minutes
Zoe	57 minutes

5 The swimming lanes are separated by strings of floats.

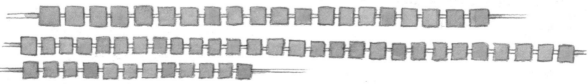

(a) Copy and complete this table for the strings of floats.

Number of green floats (g)	Number of blue floats (b)
5	

(b) Write a formula for **b** using **g**. b =

(c) Use your formula to find **b** when
• g = 10 • g = 21 • g = 32

Ice Palace

Skating	adult	£2·87
	child	£2·15
Skate hire		£1·35

1 Find the cost of skating and skate hire for

(a) 3 adults

(b) 5 children

(c) 4 adults and 3 children.

2 This is a sketch of the ice rink.

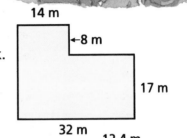

14 m

←8 m

17 m

32 m

(a) Calculate
   • the perimeter   • the area   of the rink.

(b) Make an accurate drawing of the
ice rink on centimetre squared
paper. Use a scale of **1 cm to 2 m**.

3 The diagram shows the size of
the Ice Palace advertising board.
It costs £5 per square metre to
advertise on the board.
Calculate the cost of a full board
advertisement.

12·4 m

6 m

4 There are 1840 adults with a yearly membership for the Water and Ice Palace.
Of these
   • 25% are skating only members
   • 60% are swimming only members
   • the rest are swimming **and** skating members.
How many adults have each type of membership?

5 These families want to skate **and** swim. Which families should take
the Family Saver? Explain.

Hamiltons

Simpsons

Walkers

Water and Ice Palace
Yearly membership

	Adult	Child
Skating only	£140	£105
Swimming only	£150	£110

Family Saver | Whole family £70 per month
Maximum: 2 adults + 3 children

Go to Workbook page 35.

Video Rental Charges

Thriller	**Comedy**	£1·50 each
Sport	**Horror**	
New Release		£2·50 each
Cartoon		50p each

Special Offer Any 4 videos for £8

1 Find the cost of renting (a) 1 New Release and 2 Thriller videos
(b) 2 Horror and 3 Cartoon videos.

2 (a) Is the Special Offer worthwhile when renting
1 New Release, 1 Cartoon and 2 Comedy videos? Explain.

(b) When would the special offer be worthwhile?

3 The graph shows AVID's rentals for one week.

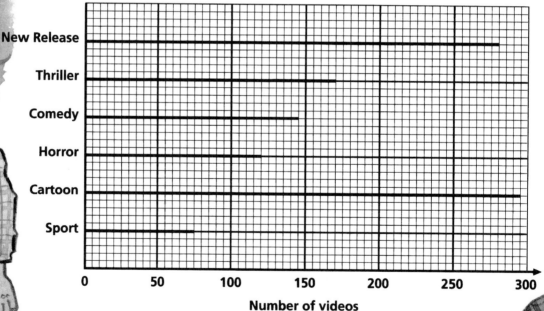

Video rentals

Number of videos

What is the maximum amount that AVID could have received
for the week's rental of

(a) Thrillers   (b) Cartoons   (c) Sport?

Problem solving **4** What is (a) the maximum   (b) the minimum amount
that AVID could receive from the rental of New Releases?

Ask your teacher what to do next.